NOW WHAT?

A Behavior Analyst's
First-Year Survival Guide

NOW WHAT?

A Behavior Analyst's
First-Year Survival Guide

Mariah Avery, MA, BCBA

KeyPress Publishing

KeyPress Publishing
www.keypresspublishing.com

KeyPress Publishing

This book is a work of nonfiction. Unless otherwise noted, the author and the publisher make no explicit guarantees as to the accuracy of the information contained in this book, and in some cases, names of people and places have been altered to protect their privacy.

Author: Mariah Avery, MA, BCBA

Now What? A Behavior Analyst's First-Year Survival Guide

Published by: KeyPress Publishing
Publisher: Alice Darnell Lattal
Brand Integrity: Lisa Smith and Jana Burtner
Production Manager: Adele Hall
Editors: Ashley Johnson and Stefanie Carr
Designers: Jana Burtner and KaCee Costello-Vargo

ISBN: 979-8-9886548-3-4

Distributed by:
ABA Technologies, Inc.
930 South Harbor City Blvd, Suite 402
Melbourne, FL 32901
www.abatechnologies.com

KeyPress Publishing books are available at a special discount for bulk purchases by corporations, institutions, and other organizations. For more information, please email keypress@abatechnologies.com.

To all the BCBA's who helped me survive my first year and beyond:
Thank you for your time, patience, and insight.

Table of Contents

Preface

Trust me, if I survived, you can too.

- I came into the field never having heard of applied behavior analysis (ABA).
- I went into graduate school having no experience in psychology.
  - Or education.
  - Or children (aside from my own and a few babysitting gigs).
- I started my fieldwork hours still not really understanding ABA.
  - Early on in my internship, my manager asked me to describe ABA. I said, "Magic." Only I was amused.

For a little context ...

I had my son during my sophomore year of college. I was in a music conservatory at the time, studying French horn. He had a bit of a rough start in life, requiring frequent hospitalizations and an open-heart surgery at 4 months old.

It's funny the things you remember from stressful times. I recall most of his first few months and almost all of his heart surgery in disjointed chunks, like a buffering video. The clearest memory I have is when they brought him from the cardiac intensive care unit to the step-down unit and the surgeon came to do the last official check-in; I remember the room smelled like an artificial lemon cleaner, the kind that burns a bit when you breathe it in, and I remember looking into the surgeon's eyes as he told me, "He [my son] will be walking, talking, and running by two."

"Walking, talking, and running by two" became my only mantra, meditation, and modicum of hope. The feeding, speech, occupational, and physical therapy started right after surgery and never stopped. After the heart issues became less pressing, the lung issues started, and we were never out of the hospital for long. I finished my bachelor's degree in music about the time he was a year old. He wasn't sitting up at that point, but I knew he would be "walking, talking, and running by two."

In retrospect, his entire therapy team must have thought I was borderline delusional. He was a few months shy of his second birthday when I realized what the surgeon had told me wasn't a prophecy—and it wasn't happening. My son wasn't walking or talking—let alone running—and was engaging in maladaptive behavior. I happened to see a video on social media of someone sharing their child's journey with autism. The similarities were undeniable. I called every psychologist's office within a 3-hour drive, and no one had availability to test him.

We ended up in a clinical trial that allowed us to get an evaluation, which was about 5 hours from our home. We left that trial with a diagnosis of autism and a prescription for full-time ABA that was impossible to fill. I called every ABA company in three states and even contacted the individuals on the Behavior Analyst Certification Board® (BACB®) Certificant Registry. Most had a waiting list that spanned a few years, all would have required private payment, and none were affordable.

I realized that it would be cheaper and faster to get a master's degree and do 1,700 hours of fieldwork to become a Board Certified Behavior Analyst® (BCBA) than it would be to self-pay for ABA. Back then, fieldwork hours were often completed via unpaid internships, so I interned 8:30 a.m.–5:00 p.m., waitressed 5:30 p.m.–11:30 p.m., worked on my online program 12:00 a.m.–2:00 a.m., and did it all over again the next day. My son was my practice partner for those first few years, and now and then I still see remnants of those early "sessions."

Once I was out of school and out of the very structured, research-focused clinical environment I had been in I felt like I had been thrown out of the frying pan and into the fire. Even worse, the fire kept judging me for not knowing things, and telling me I didn't work quickly enough. I had no idea how to apply ABA in practical terms in other settings; what an Individualized Education Program (IEP) was; how to do an assessment; and most important, why no one was using the words I'd just spent 2 years learning. Thankfully I had some cool people along the way who were able to pick me up, put out the fires, and show me what to do. I learned to become a competent behavior analyst, and my son learned to walk, talk, and run.

This book is the tool I wish I had, and my way of picking you up, dusting you off, making sure you are okay and stay that way. Even if we have come to this point from different places and for different reasons, I survived, and you can too.

Introduction

Hi and welcome! Thanks for picking up this book. Before you get any further, I want to clarify something: This isn't your typical professional development book. You won't find a list of learning directives or active student responding opportunities (ASRs). Instead, you'll find journal prompts, jargon crosswords, and scheduling sudoku. Going from a graduate student to an ABA practitioner can be like jumping into the Arctic Ocean; the shock to the system is overwhelming. The intention of this book is to help you get yourself out of the water and warm up a bit.

Journal Prompts

There are journal prompts throughout the book, with larger sections at the beginning and end. Take a few minutes to complete these as you encounter them, and then look back on them after you've completed the book.

Chapters

The chapter topics were selected based on struggles I had during my first year, mixed with frequently asked questions I have heard from my supervisees. The chapters are made of a mix of content, personal stories, and interactive elements to help you apply and unwind after a long day of behavior-analyzing. They are short and intended for easy review and reference.

Activities, Exercises, and Tools

Throughout the chapters, you'll find Activities, Exercises, and Tools. Activities are intended to be fun ways to apply concepts from the chapter. Exercises are intended to be short breaks for you to reflect/take action on chapter content. Tools are intended for you to bookmark for when you need them later.

Glossary and Appendix

Whoa, did your supervisor just use an acronym you've never heard before? Quick—check the glossary to get an idea of what they meant. And if that acronym stands for a screening or assessment tool, you can then head to the appendix for a quick reference guide on the most common of those tools.

Before You Begin

These early days will feel jam-packed from start to end, yet they'll be over in the blink of an eye. Stop and take a few moments to respond to these questions to capture and reflect on the feelings of your early journey in the field.

What made you decide to become a behavior analyst?

What areas would you like to grow in?

What are you looking forward to doing?

What hesitations do you have going into your work as a behavior analyst?

What are your goals for your future work as a behavior analyst?

CHAPTER 1

Sorting Out Scheduling

A schedule (calendar, timetable, diary, agenda book, whatever you want to call it) is, at its heart, a basic time management tool. The purpose is to organize when tasks/events/actions/activities take place. Seems easy, right? Not quite. As a behavior analyst, you will need to schedule your supervisions, caregiver trainings, client sessions, treatment planning, staff training, assessments and reassessments, and anything else that comes up. If I had 199 problems in clinical practice, the schedule definitely accounted for at least half of them.

In short, you need a work schedule where all relevant people can see changes and you can reference it when the need to schedule or make changes comes up. It doesn't matter that a correct schedule exists if not everyone is seeing it.

That is the issue I had with my system. I had a pocket-sized calendar book I took with me everywhere. I lived for the color coding and stickers. Since no one else could see it, I tended to get double-booked because the office manager referenced my client-facing calendar when scheduling appointments on my behalf. We eventually switched to something shared and digital so that, with cell phones, we could all have the same calendar in the palm of our hands. Pro tip: If your schedule includes client-specific information, make sure it meets all privacy and Health Insurance Portability and Accountability Act (HIPAA) guidelines.

You may have someone assisting you with your work schedule, like I did, especially with client-facing tasks. Be sure to maintain open lines of communication with them about what to prioritize and when. Double-booking will happen, and everyone who is touching the schedule needs to know the hierarchy of events. My supervision would constantly get overridden to cover client direct services. Be proactive and communicate directly about the circumstances in which overriding or double-booking is and is not okay for the scheduling team to do.

If personal appointments come up, you do not necessarily need to disclose the nature of the appointment, but you do need to confirm when and for how long you need to be off the schedule. Providing this information in advance will help preserve a healthy collaboration with the person who is helping to maintain your schedule.

MANAGING YOUR PERSONAL AND PROFESSIONAL SCHEDULES

Flexible schedules are a blessing and a curse. I have always had a hard time balancing work and life when presented with flexible/nontraditional work hours. Here are a few things that have helped me along the way.

1. Set a regular time to update your personal calendar with everyone's schedule (e.g., children, significant others), and put everything on it. To make sure I include everything, I think about and group calendar items into categories like this:

    - social time (lunches/family and friend obligations)
    - alone time (for me this means over-the-top Korean romantic dramas, with no one speaking to me)
    - workouts/health appointments/time-sensitive medications
    - life maintenance (car appointments, grocery shopping)
    - "flex" (flexible) time for things that inevitably come up in work or private life

2. Make sure it is accurate from that day through about 2 months in the future. Some of these appointments will change, but the majority will be the same. This will prevent double-booking.

    - Things I have managed to double-book over the years:
      - caregiver trainings
      - car appointments and doctor's appointments
      - direct client service and supervision sessions

3. Have access to your personal calendar during work hours. As a behavior analyst, you will be scheduling supervision sessions, caregiver meetings, staff training, and administrative tasks. Depending on your position and work environment, these may or may not fall into traditional working hours.

    - Again, you do not need to tell the entire office when you have a doctor's appointment, car appointment, or scream-singing-in-your-car-to-relieve-frustration appointment. Just block that off as paid time off (PTO) or personal time, depending on your organization's policies.

HOW TO MAKE IT ALL FIT: DIVIDE LARGE TASKS INTO SMALLER ONES

In addition to adding all the actual events to my schedule, I find it helpful to schedule blocks of time for getting work done in between all those events (meetings, trainings, appointments, etc.). When it comes to completing tasks like typical treatment plans and reports (and others that have due dates far in the future), I like to break the task into subgoals and schedule my time blocks accordingly. Breaking things up helps me continue to achieve small goals, without being so overwhelmed at the time of the deadline.

Pay attention to how long these smaller tasks take. This will help you plan enough time in the future. You can keep a written log or use a time-tracking application to monitor how much time you spend doing different things. Think of it as a self-monitoring program. You can even graph it if it makes you feel warm and fuzzy.

Once you know where you spend your time, you can think about whether you need to change anything or become more efficient by restructuring.

You can break a big task into smaller ones in a few different ways:

- divide it into categories
- order it sequentially (e.g., the first page of the report first)
- divide it by mental effort (e.g., what can be multitasked, what requires your full attention)

Here's how I might use this approach to set up for a discrete trial training (DTT) session. When I first started running my own schedule, I never gave myself any time to set up my sessions. I overbooked myself, and it made me a flustered mess when sessions started. I'm using setting up for a session as an illustrative example, but these methods will apply to anything else you may need to schedule (paperwork, administrative tasks, etc.).

Divide it into categories
Example categories: DTT cards (specific to the client), reinforcers, tools (data sheet, clickers)

Order it sequentially
Example sequence: transition materials, first-probe-round materials, teaching-round-1 materials, etc.

Divide it by mental effort
Low effort: cards
Rationale: I can receive a report from the previous therapist while doing this part of the task.

Medium effort: tools
Rationale: I need to find the clickers because no one ever puts them back in the same place.

High effort: reinforcers
Rationale: I'll need to scope out some of the new toys that came in yesterday and see if my client might like them. Some of the reinforcers they usually go for may have been used and need to be wiped down. I'll also need to get edibles from the kitchen.

🎯 EXERCISE 1.1:   BREAKING UP A TASK

Now it's your turn to break up a bigger task. Take a task you do every day, and break it down by using each of these methods.

Divide it into categories:

Order it sequentially:

Divide it by mental effort:

MEETINGS

As a behavior analyst, you are going to have a lot of meetings on your schedule, with all different kinds of people. First, let's break them up into general meeting types.

General Meeting Types

1. **The Update**
   - This meeting is interactive, where each party involved has information to share with the others. Think of this like getting together with someone you haven't seen for a while—you take turns sharing what you've been up to.

2. **The Infodump**
   - This is the classic should-have-been-an email meeting. One party provides information to the other parties, and response/input from the other parties is not required.

3. **The Decider**
   - This is a meeting where people come together with the intention to make decisions/solve a problem. These can be long (and heated) because they usually come up when there is a problem.

4. **The Boost**
   - This is a team-building meeting, although they don't always have this effect.

Calling a Meeting

Now that you know about the types of meetings and how they may apply to your clinical practice, we can get into the when and how. Meetings can be a time suck, and having too many of them can destroy even the most carefully crafted schedule; but they can be great for communicating information and collective problem-solving. In my opinion, if it takes more than three emails, it should be a meeting—but if the meeting would take less than 15 minutes, you should try it as an email.

In my opinion, if it takes more than three emails, it should be a meeting—but if the meeting would take less than 15 minutes, you should try it as an email.

⚡ ACTIVITY 1.1: MEETING TYPE MATCH

Instructions: As a behavior analyst, you will routinely have meetings with caregivers, members of your own team, and other service providers (more on that in Chapter 9). See if you can identify what type each meeting description might fall into. *See p. 145 to check your answers!*

Word bank: The Update, The Infodump, The Decider, The Boost

Caregiver/adult client meetings (external meetings):

_____   Reviewing policies, procedures, and expectations

_____   Treatment plan updates (reviewing progress)

_____   Client/caregiver not in compliance with policy

_____ and/or _____   Conducting typical caregiver training sessions

_____ and/or _____   A new problem behavior has occurred

Team meetings (internal meetings):

_____   A policy has changed

_____ and/or _____   A client is engaging in new problem behavior

_____ and/or _____   A routine check-in about a client's progress

Meetings with other professionals (internal meetings):

_____ and/or _____   The client has begun a new maladaptive behavior

_____ and/or _____   The client is not making the expected progress

_____   A regularly scheduled meeting about a client

☀ TOOL 1.1: DO WE NEED A MEETING?

Instructions: Before scheduling a meeting, ask yourself these questions:

Does it need to be *had*?	Yes / No
Does it need to be had *by me*?	Yes / No
Does it need to be had by me *now*?	Yes / No

It needs to be had, but not by you, and not now.

This is a good opportunity to bring in a meeting facilitator who is a master in the topic at hand. Think about who might be the best person to deliver the information, assist in resolving the issue, or build team spirit, and reach out to them. I did this once when morale in one of my clinics was low and we needed a boost meeting. Now, I could have run the boost meeting, but since I had the time to plan, I connected with our company's other clinic in the region, and we held a combined boost meeting. The director at that clinic had much more experience with boost meetings, so I asked him to take the lead. Instead of running the meeting, I took care of other needs like snacks, supplies, and general coordination.

It needs to be had, by you, but not now.

You have the gift of time. Thoughtfully plan out what needs to be said and how, and anticipate any questions or pain points that might come up. Plan an agenda and any additional resources related to the meeting topic.

It needs to be had, by you, and now.

My first recommendation is for you to take a breath. Check in with your emotions, and think about why you are having this meeting. In my experience, these meetings tend to come up around conflict, impasse, or other issues. Yes, any kind of corrective feedback should be given in the moment, and problems are best solved sooner rather than later, but keep in mind that few problems are solved when emotions and adrenaline are high. You won't be able to control the emotions of the other meeting parties, but you can make sure that you are in a cool-calm-and-collected headspace.

Scheduling Meetings

You should try to schedule meetings at natural transition times to reduce task-switching time. Task switching is the time it takes to redirect your attention from one task to another and get refocused. Task-switching time can drain anywhere from an extra 10–50 minutes from the day (Mark, 2023). Natural transition times will look different at every organization, but think of them as times you (and your colleagues) would change tasks anyway. At one of my first clinic-based jobs, we had 2-hour sessions, so the staff was in transition every 2 hours. I tended to book meetings in those blocks as well, so that my supervision schedule wasn't fighting against my meeting schedule.

On days with successive meetings, try to end a meeting at least 10 minutes before the start of the next one to ensure people have time to gracefully transition to the next one (e.g., take bathroom and coffee breaks). It sounds counterintuitive, but it will help you start your next meeting on time. Also keep in mind how far apart you schedule these meetings. If you only have 30 minutes or an hour between meetings, that is not likely to be productive time.

⊚ EXERCISE 1.2:   TRACKING TRANSITIONS

Bring a stopwatch or use a timing app to see how much time you spend transitioning in a given day:

How much of that time was related to transitions between meetings?

Even if your transitions are on point, meetings may still be a huge barrier to productivity.

To make sure you get the most out of your meetings, try the following:

- make agendas,
- send out said agendas ahead of time, and
- send out action items after the meeting with dates for them to be accomplished.

SURVIVAL BASICS

A clear and well-managed schedule is a cornerstone to surviving as a behavior analyst. Staying on top of your schedule and being mindful of everyone's time when it comes to meetings will go a long way to keeping you on track, this year and beyond.

Scheduling Sudoku

By the end of this you may be saying, "But Mariah, you still haven't told me how I can get better at scheduling." If you want to get better at scheduling, get reasonably good at sudoku. You can't convince me they aren't the same thing, or that they don't both use the same parts of your brain (probably). Think about it like this:

- Every square has to contain a single number: You can only do one thing at a time.
- Only the numbers 1–9 can be used: You only have about 8 hours in a workday, plus lunch.
- Every box/row/column must have one instance each of numbers 1–9: You have a certain number of tasks that must get done each day.

✒ ACTIVITY 1.2: SCHEDULING SUDOKU

Instructions: List your own tasks for the upcoming week, and then play sudoku with those tasks in mind. *See p. 146 for the answer key to check your scheduling prowess!*

1.

2.

3.

4.

5.

6.

7.

8.

9.

	8	7	3		5	2	1	4
	2			4	1	8	9	
6	1		8	9	2		7	5
1				8		7		
	9	2			7		8	
5				3	6		4	
		1		7		5		8
7	6	3			8			1
8	5		1	2	3		6	7

CHAPTER 2

Dazzling With Data

You dealt with data during your training: taking and graphing it. Now that you're a certified behavior analyst, the process doesn't change as much as the volume and level of responsibility.

A NOTE ABOUT THE STANDARD CELERATION CHART

Now, you may or may not have experience using the *Standard Celeration Chart* (SCC), sometimes called the standard behavior chart (Kubina, 2015). I've never used an SCC in clinical practice, nor have I worked directly with anyone who has used these charts. At the writing of this chapter, the best guesstimate is that about 3% of behavioral agencies use SCCs (R. Kubina, personal communication, November 28, 2022). We can't know for sure because no one has answered that question through research, but adjacent questions have been answered. In case you've found yourself in one of those agencies, or would like to, here's a very basic introduction.

Celeration charts are Skinner approved: "The curve revealed things in the rate of responding, and changes in that rate, which would certainly otherwise have been missed" (Skinner, 1956, p. 225).

In full disclosure, I had to have SCCs explained to me no fewer than 20 times before I understood the concept. The data are plotted on what looks like graph paper, but the axes work a bit differently from linear graph axes. It isn't overly complicated—the issue was me.

My fieldwork experience placed a big focus on frequency (or count). I had a hard time understanding rate as anything different from frequency. I'm not the best person to explain this in detail, but I can share how it was explained to me in a way that finally made it stick.

If I tell you the number of miles driven by a car (100) and the amount of time it took (2 hours), you can figure out the rate after the fact (50 mph), but that rate may not be accurate. Maybe they were going 75 mph, stopped off for a bathroom break, and then did their best *Fast & Furious* impression at the end. Looking at a standardized measure of rate shows you the speedometer of the car as you are driving so that you can make in-the-moment decisions.

If you'd like to really dig into SCCs, I recommend checking out the great video series from the Standard Celeration Society (n.d.).

DATA SHEETS

I have worked primarily with data sheets in my ABA career. At the writing of this chapter, you're more likely to find yourself in an agency that uses data sheets. Here are a few things to keep in mind:

- The data you collect should answer a question. When making a data sheet, ask yourself, "What do I want to know?" Try to limit yourself to two questions if the person collecting the data is outside the field of ABA. Here are some examples of two-question sets
  - When did it happen, and how bad was it?
  - What happened before, and how long did it last?
- If it takes your data collector more than 10 seconds to fill out your sheet, it's too complicated and they won't do it. Or worse, they'll fudge it.
  - If no one is filling out your data sheet, simplify it.
    - I don't have any data to support this, but in my experience, the less "busy" the data sheet looks, the more data I've received. Complicated sheets worked okay in a clinic, but once I sent them out into the non-ABA world, it was just too much to do and too much to look at for the data takers.
  - Consider the entire data-taking process from start to finish and keep it simple.
    - Once, early on in my career, I had a situation where a caregiver just stopped taking data. This was an old-school data binder in a group-home setting. I had been in this setting for over a year at this point and had a really good relationship with the house manager. I asked her to level with me: "Is it the data sheet? Have I upset anyone?" She told me they liked the sheets, and I hadn't managed to burn any bridges. However, because of another client's behavior plan, they had to store the pens away from where they kept the binders. That made recording the data a pain. I went to the store later that day and bought a pack of soft, felt tip markers. After that I had very brightly colored, but full, data sheets.
    - Another time. I wanted duration for a behavior that was occurring in a different group home. I tried for months. I did training, but it just wasn't feasible

for staff to sit there with a timer. Looking back, I'm genuinely impressed that the staff tried so hard to appease me on this. I then turned it into checkboxes: < 30 minutes, 30–45 minutes, 46–60 minutes, > 60 minutes. This allowed them to look at the clock when they saw the event and look at it after everything settled back down. I was able to track the reduction in time that way, roughly. It was messy, but it answered the question.

- If your data collector doesn't like you, they probably won't take data.
  - This one is self-explanatory. Taking data is often seen as a favor for the person asking for it. This is something I tend to lean in to: "I know the ABC [Antecedent-Behavior-Consequence] data is a little more intense than the tally sheet, but I would really appreciate it if you could complete it. I think there is more going on than the tally sheet is telling me." And, of course, just be nice.
- If you are the kind of person who gets joy from beautiful data sheets, I applaud you. I was once just like you, but then I gave up.
  - Once, I spent forever making cute, themed data sheets for self-monitoring. I excitedly presented these to my client, just for the client to look at me and say, "I want it plain."

◎ EXERCISE 2.1:   SIMPLIFY IT

Take a program you utilize with a client and see if you can reduce it to something that is (a) a series of checkboxes or (b) something that can be entered *after* the fact.

◎ EXERCISE 2.2:   TEMPLATE TIME

Save clean copies of data sheets that you make, without any identifying information. You should have these templates in your collection. Check them off as you go.

☐ ABC data collection

☐ Checklist-style task analysis

☐ A frequency/count sheet (daily, weekly, monthly)

☐ A cold-probe-style sheet

☐ A trial-by-trial-style sheet

☐ An observation recording sheet

- As a behavior analyst, you can count on needing to observe. I prefer to use data sheets so that I'm not trying to make sense of a bunch of tally marks on notebook paper.

☐ A goal-tracking sheet (what are the goals, what have we met, and what needs to be worked on)

- This one is usually met with some resistance when I share it with new behavior analysts. Imagine 10 goals per client—because the math is easy, not because that is a benchmark of some kind. Now imagine 10 children. I've almost always had more clients than that at any point in time. That's 100 goals. Throw in that each of these goals will be changing/updating at different points; you will need a way to keep track of what you are currently working on.

☐ Other:

☐ Other:

RAW DATA: PAPER

If you use data sheets, you will need to take care of them. If a paper data sheet were a pet, it would be a really high-maintenance pet, not something easy like a goldfish. Paper data sheets need to be kept under conditions that are HIPAA compliant. There are workarounds (e.g., if your data sheet doesn't have any client information on it), but it's better to be overly cautious than risk a privacy breach. If you work in or with schools, you should be aware of the Family Educational Rights and Privacy Act (FERPA) and how it may impact your data collection procedures. I like to think of FERPA as HIPAA for schools.

◎ EXERCISE 2.3: MY DATA MANAGEMENT REQUIREMENTS

Each organization will have unique policies for data management and protection. Fill in your organization's requirements here.

I need to keep data for _____ [months] [years]

My paper data will be stored permanently in _____

The HIPAA policies around paper data are _____

If I work with schools, I will comply with FERPA by _____

_____

If I lose paper data, I contact _____

RAW DATA: DIGITAL

You can also collect data digitally through programs that meet all the required privacy guidelines. I have had the opportunity to use a few different ones myself. If your organization utilizes one of these programs, I recommend actually watching the instructional videos that come with the program. In one job, I watched the entire backlog of instructional videos and became my company's guru for that program. Being fluent in the software made my job so much easier and allowed me to help others in the organization.

🎯 EXERCISE 2.4:   LOOK IT UP

Take a moment to look up and watch, or at least bookmark, the relevant instructions for your organization's program (if applicable).

GRAPHS

Now that you have the data, what do you do with it? Well, you graph it of course.

If you are using self-graphing software, this is done for you. If not, you will need to learn to graph in Microsoft Excel. The good news is that there are many resources out there.

Carr and Burkholder (1998) published a step-by-step guide: "Creating Single-Subject Design Graphs With Microsoft Excel™."

There is also a replication and revision for those of us who use a more updated version of Excel: "Creating Single-Subject Design Graphs in Microsoft Excel 2007" (Dixon et al., 2009).

There are also a ton of ABA Excel tutorials on YouTube. I'm a visual person, so I utilized these early on. Though the ones that I used are no longer available, there are surely current ones you could search for if videos are helpful for you.

If you are going to use Excel, I would strongly recommend using templates. You'll spend more time in the beginning setting up the templates, but overall, it will save you time. How you save an Excel sheet as a template will vary depending on which version of Excel you have. For a specific how-to guide, check out Microsoft (n.d.).

Official vs. Everyday Graphs

As a field, we strive for consistency. In graduate school, you learned the correct way to make graphs for use in the field. The *Journal of Applied Behavior Analysis* (*JABA*) also has clear guidelines on how your graphs should look for publication (JABA, n.d.). There are too many guidelines to list, but some relate to coloring, the aspect ratio of the axes, and the shape of data points. If you graph per industry standards, you will save yourself a step should you ever choose to submit anything for publication.

That said, I've always found that it's difficult for caregivers and stakeholders to read the industry-standard graphs. It's a lot of black and a lot of phase lines. I've tended to use official graphs for official purposes, and the graphs that best answer the question for unofficial purposes.

A Warning on Graphs

It is easy to "lie" with graphs, especially unintentionally. One stretched axis, and you have completely changed the slope of your line. Darrell Huff's *How to Lie with Statistics* (1954/1993) should be on your reading list this year. Huff describes the ways in which we can unwittingly misrepresent our data more eloquently than I ever could.

How Often Should You Be Graphing?

Overall, your graphs should be referred to as often as possible and updated as often as possible. This means no less than monthly, and you really shouldn't be making major programming decisions without consulting your graphs. Technology is here to help with that.

Basic office applications like Excel, or Numbers, can do more than you think. You can create templates for data entry that feed into graphs. These will automatically update as you enter data (as long as you set them up that way). You can link said graphs to slide presentations for stakeholders and have them automatically update as the graphs do.

Taking it a step further, I'm currently trying to learn some basic computer programming. I'm pretty convinced that it will be the next frontier for data analysis in ABA. What takes a few hours to set up in Excel can be done in minutes when utilizing a programming language.

Graphing Bloopers

Everyone has a "whoops" story around graphing. Literally every behavior analyst has managed to make some mistakes in this area. Here are a few:

- This story is shared with Jason's permission. Jason and I became BCBAs at the same time. He hadn't graphed anything for an entire treatment plan because he didn't know how to use Excel and was too embarrassed to ask. Instead, he was mastering them out (marking skills as complete) on the raw data sheet and sketching graphs in the margins. The whole thing came to a head when it was time to turn in graphs to the insurance company and Jason had to explain to our mutual boss and the admin team that there were no graphs. Jason still needed graphs for the treatment plan to be submitted, so he had to pull an all-nighter to graph all the data he had taken.

- Once, I was presenting on my clients in a Local Review Committee. If you haven't experienced this yet, it's where you go over your programming with a team of senior behavior analysts, not just from your company, but local BCBAs as well. In this particular instance, I was printing out graphs as other people were presenting. It was an absolute mess, but that isn't the best (or worst) part of the story. I had been given an Excel template that had five series on it, meaning that it was set up to graph five behaviors. I only needed to graph four, but I couldn't figure out how to delete the extra series. Instead, I put a really high number in series five so it would look much higher than the other four. From there, I was supposed to right-click the data point and delete it. Well, I forgot the deleting part as I was scrambling to print, so I handed over a graph that looked like my client did some mystery behavior 50 times in a single day. I tried to explain myself, but I couldn't really get out an explanation—I was too nervous and embarrassed. I think I just kept repeating, "It's not real," which wasn't informative. I ended up needing to re-present the next quarter, and thankfully someone showed me how to deselect a series before then.

- Once, I couldn't figure out how to get a digital data collection tool to do anything but trial-by-trial data. My company at the time did cold-probe-style data, so I tried changing the goals over to a trial-by-trial format. It was a massive undertaking that just blew up in my face, as some technicians defaulted to cold-probe and others collected trial-by-trial data. I ended up doing so much unnecessary work, when I should have reached out for help, either to the digital data collection company itself or to someone more familiar with that software at my company.

- Add some of your own!

SURVIVAL BASICS

As a behavior analyst, you will eat, sleep, and breathe data. Remember to:

- Know the privacy guidelines of your organization and what the applicable laws are (HIPAA/FERPA).

- Find additional resources on the graphing methods you are currently using at your organization (digital collection methods, graphing in Excel). That way, you have them if and when you need them.

- Not reinvent the wheel: Keep any data sheets, graph templates, or target programs you developed in a digital data collection software. It is often easier to modify something you already have than to start over each time.

- Make data sheets, trackers, and graphs (if you are feeling fancy) for your own use outside of work with a client. Your tools aren't just for clients!

CHAPTER 3

Assessment Lineup

ABA is full of questionnaires and assessments of all kinds. Let's talk about what you should expect to see and what you'll need to do with it. The assessments in this chapter appear in the order in which a child and their caregiver(s) would come into contact with them. This should give you an overall understanding of what they've likely encountered before making it to you. Note that references and links for all screenings and assessments listed in this chapter can be found in the Appendix.

DEVELOPMENTAL MONITORING

All caregivers are encouraged to monitor their child's development with the help of their pediatrician, along with handouts from the Centers for Disease Control and Prevention (CDC). This collaborative monitoring may lead to the identification of developmental delays that could lead to diagnoses. It's important to note that not everyone who has delayed milestones will have any further diagnoses or exceptionalities. As a behavior analyst, you are not likely to be a part of this process, although you technically could fill out these handouts in collaboration with the caregivers.

DEVELOPMENTAL SCREENING

Educators and pediatricians, in combination with caregivers, fill out developmental screenings (or "screeners") to see if the child is a candidate for further evaluation or services. These screeners are meant to be brief snapshots of the child and do not replace a comprehensive evaluation. I've filled out these a few times when I was contracting with early education facilities. While you may never be asked to fill out a screener personally, you may receive copies when doing an assessment or working with young children.

Common Developmental Screeners

1. Ages & Stages Questionnaires® (ASQ®)
2. Ages & Stages Questionnaires: Social-Emotional (ASQ:SE)
3. BRIGANCE® Screens
4. Developmental Assessment of Young Children (DAYC)
5. Early Screening Profiles (ESP)
6. Learning Accomplishment Profile™-Diagnostic (LAP™-D)
7. Parents' Evaluation of Developmental Status (PEDS®)
8. Parents' Evaluation of Developmental Status: Developmental Milestones (PEDS:DM®)

A comprehensive list of screeners can be found on the CDC website, with resources on how to interpret the results (Centers for Disease Control and Prevention, 2023). However, in your role, you are not likely to need to research or perform these unless you are asked by a caregiver or a school. From the list above, I have personally encountered the Ages & Stages Questionnaires most often, usually during client intake. Although some clients will come to you with screening results, you shouldn't expect that all clients will.

DIAGNOSTIC ASSESSMENTS

If the developmental screening proved to be noteworthy, the child will likely be referred to a diagnosing provider. At the writing of this chapter, there is a large shortage of these professionals, and the wait times can be long. There are a variety of providers that can diagnose, including multidisciplinary panels.

A few diagnosing providers you are likely to encounter:

- developmental pediatrician
- pediatric neurologist
- child psychologist
- child psychiatrist

It is up to the individual provider which assessments or combination of assessments they would like to use. They then provide reports that they feel most accurately represent the client.

Similar to behavior analysts, these providers also have some payor requirements (more on those in Chapter 4) that may impact the assessments or types of assessments they use. For example, at the writing of this chapter, Georgia Medicaid has begun requiring that a caregiver interview tool be part of every diagnostic evaluation for autism.

You are most likely to encounter these developmental assessments and tools in the context of diagnostic evaluations when you receive a new client, or when a current client receives an updated evaluation. These reports will provide context and interpretation for their respective scores.

Common Diagnostic Assessments for Autism

1. Autism Diagnostic Interview (ADI®): A caregiver interview

2. Autism Diagnostic Observation Schedule™ (ADOS®): An observation-based assessment

3. Mullen Scales of Early Learning: A standardized assessment across developmental areas

4. Vineland Adaptive Behavior Scales: A caregiver interview that can also be administered by a behavior analyst as a part of an ABA evaluation

The *Diagnostic and Statistical Manual of Mental Disorders* (DSM)

The *Diagnostic and Statistical Manual of Mental Disorders* (*DSM*) was first published in 1952. It serves as a reference guide for diagnosing providers and is published by the American Psychiatric Association (APA). The *DSM* has symptoms, basic descriptions, and diagnosis criteria for a wide variety of mental health disorders. It also contains statistics such as the age of onset and risk factors. It should be noted that the *DSM* has been updated multiple times, with the expectation of continued updates to reflect the most up-to-date information. Certain diagnoses have been removed or modified in new editions as deemed appropriate by the APA. Although as a behavior analyst you are not considered a diagnosing provider and should make no attempts to diagnose or insinuate potential diagnoses to a client, you can use this manual to learn about any comorbid conditions your client may experience. Prior to reviewing, make sure you have the most up-to-date edition, which at the writing of this chapter is the *DSM-5-TR* (American Psychiatric Association, 2022).

ASSESSMENTS USED IN ABA

An ABA assessment can be conducted as an independent measure (i.e., without coordination with other providers) or as part of the client's multidisciplinary team. At the writing of this chapter, there are common assessments that you should have some familiarity with. Certain payors and organizations will have strong preferences when it comes to what assessments are used. These assessments are not limited to ABA in their use.

1. Early Start Denver Model (ESDM)

   • This assessment is designed for younger children, 12–60 months old. It was developed by Drs. Sally Rogers and Geraldine Dawson.

2. Verbal Behavior Milestones Assessment and Placement Program (VB-MAPP)

   • The VB-MAPP is based on Skinner's *Verbal Behavior* (1957) and developed its benchmarking based on typical language development in young children. Each level corresponds to a developmental range. It was developed by Dr. Mark L. Sundberg.

3. Assessment of Basic Language and Learning Skills, Revised (ABLLS-R®)

   • These skills include visual performance, response to reinforcement, expressive/receptive communication, social play, group responding, and imitation. The assessment was developed by Dr. James W. Partington.

4. Promoting Emergence of Advanced Knowledge (PEAK)

   • The PEAK assessment assesses cognition and language skills. The four modules in this assessment are Generalization, Direct Training, Equivalence, and Transformation. It was developed by Dr. Mark Dixon.

5. Essential for Living (EFL)

   • This is a skills assessment, curriculum, and skill-tracking instrument for children as well as adults with mild-to-severe disabilities. It was developed by Dr. Patrick McGreevy.

6. Assessment of Functional Living Skills (AFLS)

   • AFLS provides a complete list of essential skills for home, living, school, community participation, vocation, and independent living. It was created by Drs. James W. Partington and Michael Mueller.

When you think about assessments, think of them more as benchmarking tools and less as checklists or to-do lists. Not every person will have every "skill" that is assigned to their age, regardless of whether a developmental disability is present. When I came out of graduate school, my only experience with developmental milestones had been working with children who experienced delays and my son's development, which also had a unique trajectory. I had no idea of the extent of natural variances and standard deviations to be found with milestones. Because of that, I didn't really know when to "stop." I would just keep checking boxes without thinking if that skill was really something an "x"-year-old should be doing.

At the recommendation of my clinical director at the time, I started volunteering at a local childcare facility for preschoolers a few hours a week. It taught me important lessons like:

1. Cleanup songs have the highest stimulus control I've ever seen—scary stuff.

   • Now having this knowledge, I started using it in my own clinical practice to ease transitions.

2. Three-year-olds start sentences having no idea how that sentence will end.

   • I stopped being so quick to prompt my clients, and when appropriate, I let them figure it out as they went along.

3. While preschool children CAN use mand frames (e.g., I want, I need, hand me, give me), they will also just walk right up to you and take things with the confidence I wish I had.

   • Mand training will always be important, but I learned not to be such a perfectionist once the skill was demonstrated to mastery.

After the experience of spending time with children who had not been identified as having developmental delays, I learned to use assessments to inform clinical decision-making without being consumed by the need to check off every skill all at once. If you are like me and up until this point haven't had much experience around a population you work with except as clientele (whether that be young children, tweens, teens, adults, or animals), I'd recommend finding a way to spend time with that population in a nonclinical setting. It helped me learn what was realistic and reasonable in order to succeed in a real-world environment. I stopped holding my clients to a higher standard than their peers. Just keep in mind that doing an observation will require planning ahead—don't just roll up and say Mariah sent you.

ASSESSING PREFERENCES AND REINFORCERS

Preference assessments evaluate what someone likes (preferences). They are extremely useful to help narrow down the field of things that are *potential* reinforcers. I've found that they can also be helpful in identifying the leisure and play activities to teach that can meaningfully impact a person's day and increase their quality of life. I've heard a lot of early practitioners incorrectly use the terms "preference assessments" and "reinforcer assessments" interchangeably. *Reinforcer assessments* evaluate what impact, if any, a stimulus has on strengthening behavior.

So, in short:

Preference assessment
= What does the subject of this assessment like?

Reinforcer assessment
= Is this stimulus strengthening behavior (i.e., functioning as a reinforcer)?

See Tables 3.1 and 3.2 on the following pages.

Preference and Reinforcer Assessments

A lot of times, preferences and reinforcers coincide nicely, but sometimes they don't. For me personally, it's more often been the latter. When I was in graduate school, there was an assignment where we had to find a behavior that we wanted to reduce in ourselves. We had to go through all the steps we would take for a client. I wanted to reduce swearing. At the time I worked with young children 8:30 a.m.–5:00 p.m. and then waitressed into the early morning hours. What happened was an interesting behavioral contrast. I never swore when working with the children, but due to the nature of my late-night waitressing job, I swore like a sailor in the kitchen of the restaurant and eventually at home and any non-work setting.

I ran my preference assessment, and while I can't remember the exact results, it was pretty aligned with my tastes—if it can be found at a certain red-and-white store, it probably hits the "target" for me. I used every one of my preferences as reinforcers in different phases of a DRL (differential reinforcement of low rates of responding), and each one failed miserably.

I was very concerned about failing the class, or worse, being a poor excuse for a behavior analyst. With support from the professor, I ended up doing a reinforcer assessment and some more investigation. It turned out that the behavior

A preference does not a reinforcer make.

was attention maintained, explaining why my tangible reinforcement had minimal impact. It was a good lesson in making sure you are choosing functionally equivalent reinforcement when possible, and that a preference does not a reinforcer make.

Common Preference Assessments

Table 3.1: *Preference Assessments*

PREFERENCE ASSESSMENT	Description	Pro	Con
Single-stimulus	• Present one item at a time, while tracking engagement and reaction.	• Great option for a client who is not able to consistently choose an object	• Often less accurate than other preference assessments
Paired-stimulus (Forced-choice)	• Present two stimuli at a time, often with randomized pairing. Have the learner choose one.	• Offers a structured method for assessing	• Requires more trials, and more of a time commitment than other preference assessments
Multiple-stimulus with replacement (MSW)	• Present three or more stimuli at a time. Have the learner choose one. Once an object is chosen, it should remain in the array.	• Can present a wide variety of options in an efficient and structured way	• The learner must be able to scan and select
Multiple-stimulus without replacement (MSWO)	• Present three or more stimuli at a time. Have the learner choose one. Once an object is chosen, it is removed from the array.	• Can quickly establish a hierarchy of reinforcers	• The removal of items may elicit problem behavior
Free Operant	• Allow the learner unrestricted access to a variety of items, things you've selected (curated) or found in the environment (naturalistic).	• Can be done while other observations are taking place (e.g., during free play in a school observation)	• May be limited in accuracy

Common Reinforcer Assessments

Table 3.2: Reinforcer Assessments

REINFORCER ASSESSMENT	Description	Pro	Con
Concurrent schedule	• Compares which reinforcer produces the highest rate of desired responding.	• The learner may freely choose between the potential reinforcers	• Doesn't provide information on the strength of the potential reinforcers
Multiple schedule	• Reinforcement provided at the same schedule but at different times. The most powerful reinforcer is the one whose sessions produce the highest rate of the desired behavior.	• Allows for a systematic comparison of reinforcers across multiple data points	• More time-consuming as it must occur across multiple sessions
Progressive-ratio	• Response requirements are increased incrementally. The reinforcers that produce the most occurrences of the desired behavior are the most reinforcing.	• Provides the most insight and highest level of nuance	• Requires more design and prep work than the other assessments

ASSESSMENTS OF BEHAVIOR FUNCTION

Speaking of functionally equivalent, there are also some assessment tools to help you in determining the function of behavior.

- Questions About Behavioral Function (QABF)
- Functional Analysis Screening Tool (FAST)

These tools help guide caregiver interviews and provide further insight into potential functions of behavior. I liked including these along with my ABC data and observations to create a more well-rounded functional behavior assessment (FBA).

SURVIVAL BASICS

For assessments, thankfully, there will always be more to learn as BCBAs continue to improve and expand on the tools we have available at the writing of this chapter. No matter which assessments/tools you end up using, think about them as a part of a larger context; don't copy-paste or teach well beyond what would be age/developmentally appropriate to the client. You are the provider; the assessment is not (even though they are pretty amazing).

ACTIVITY 3.1: ASSESSMENT GRIDS

Instructions: Back in my day, aside from walking uphill both ways, we filled out assessment grids by hand with markers. Now this can be done on apps or in Excel. In honor of the old days, here is a throwback grid for you to fill out.

In the table below, you see a row with a score and date for the "1st test." Pick a color for that test date and add it in the space provided in the "Color" column. Next, look at the data set labeled "Testing 1/23/23". Domains 1–9 line up with the larger grid, and skills line up with the 1–12 on the y-axis. If you see a plus (+) like in domain 1 skill 1, color in the corresponding section of the blank table. A colored section means the learner demonstrates that skill. If there is a minus (−), leave that blank. This loosely represents assessing a learner before a period of treatment. *See p. 146 to check your answers.*

KEY	SCORE	DATE	COLOR	TESTER
1st Test	85/108	1/23/23		MA

Domain 1 Domain 2 Domain 3 Domain 4 Domain 5 Domain 6 Domain 7 Domain 8 Domain 9

Testing 1/23/23

Domain 1		Domain 2		Domain 3	
Skill 1	✚	Skill 1	✚	Skill 1	✚
Skill 2	✚	Skill 2	✚	Skill 2	✚
Skill 3	✚	Skill 3	✚	Skill 3	✚
Skill 4	✚	Skill 4	✚	Skill 4	✚
Skill 5	✚	Skill 5	✚	Skill 5	✚
Skill 6	✚	Skill 6	✚	Skill 6	✚
Skill 7	✚	Skill 7	✚	Skill 7	▬
Skill 8	✚	Skill 8	✚	Skill 8	▬
Skill 9	✚	Skill 9	✚	Skill 9	▬
Skill 10	✚	Skill 10	✚	Skill 10	▬
Skill 11	✚	Skill 11	✚	Skill 11	✚
Skill 12	✚	Skill 12	✚	Skill 12	✚

Domain 4		Domain 5		Domain 6	
Skill 1	✚	Skill 1	✚	Skill 1	✚
Skill 2	✚	Skill 2	✚	Skill 2	✚
Skill 3	✚	Skill 3	✚	Skill 3	✚
Skill 4	✚	Skill 4	✚	Skill 4	✚
Skill 5	✚	Skill 5	▬	Skill 5	✚
Skill 6	▬	Skill 6	▬	Skill 6	▬
Skill 7	▬	Skill 7	▬	Skill 7	▬
Skill 8	▬	Skill 8	▬	Skill 8	▬
Skill 9	▬	Skill 9	▬	Skill 9	▬
Skill 10	▬	Skill 10	✚	Skill 10	▬
Skill 11	✚	Skill 11	✚	Skill 11	✚
Skill 12	✚	Skill 12	✚	Skill 12	✚

Domain 7		Domain 8		Domain 9	
Skill 1	✚	Skill 1	✚	Skill 1	✚
Skill 2	✚	Skill 2	✚	Skill 2	✚
Skill 3	✚	Skill 3	✚	Skill 3	✚
Skill 4	✚	Skill 4	✚	Skill 4	✚
Skill 5	✚	Skill 5	✚	Skill 5	✚
Skill 6	✚	Skill 6	✚	Skill 6	✚
Skill 7	▬	Skill 7	✚	Skill 7	✚
Skill 8	▬	Skill 8	✚	Skill 8	✚
Skill 9	▬	Skill 9	✚	Skill 9	✚
Skill 10	▬	Skill 10	✚	Skill 10	✚
Skill 11	✚	Skill 11	✚	Skill 11	✚
Skill 12	✚	Skill 12	✚	Skill 12	✚

CHAPTER 4

Let's Talk About Funding

ABA and insurance do not have a long history, even though it may seem like it. In my time in the field, I have seen a complete overhaul of insurance expectations and requirements. I can say two things with absolute certainty: Insurance is overcomplicated (in my opinion), and as soon as you start to get a feel for what to expect, it will change.

When I was seeking ABA services for my son, 6 years before the writing of this chapter, there wasn't an approved provider for Medicaid in a three-state radius of my family home. Now there are six within a 2-hour drive.

I have written this chapter several times over. Each time, it seems to devolve into the rantings of a conspiracy theorist with a corkboard. In the interest of keeping things coherent, I am going to be very general. There are many distinct types of insurance. This is meant to give you a general idea and does not represent any individual payor.

PAYOR MANUALS

The first thing you need to know is that dealing with insurance is an open-book test. The insurance company publishes a manual that tells you what you can and cannot do, and what they will pay for. These manuals are free to access and can usually be found online at the respective company's website. If you work for an ABA provider as a clinician, odds are you will have the information from this manual regurgitated to you in easier-to-understand portions by

> *The first thing you need to know is that dealing with insurance is an open-book test. The insurance company publishes a manual that tells you what you can and cannot do, and what they will pay for.*

an angel of a person at your organization. Be sure to thank whoever that author is and read all their insurance-related communications. It is still a good idea to look at these manuals yourself—you as a provider have a lot at stake to do things correctly.

CREDENTIALING

Before you can be an approved provider for an insurance company, you need to fill out paperwork. What paperwork will change, but there will be paperwork. It boils down to two basic questions: Who are you, and are you qualified to perform this service? Most clinical companies have someone in-house dedicated to the back-and-forth with the insurance company, but you will still need to fill out your own *credentialing packet*. When I was a brand-new BCBA, a group of us met at a fast-food restaurant and filled out our paperwork together. In retrospect, we had massive amounts of personal information open in a public space—it was not the best idea—but it made the chore a lot more fun. It took about 3 hours, but we got it done! Shortly after, a member of that group got married and she opted to keep her maiden name, in part, to avoid having to redo that paperwork.

CRACK THE CODES

Insurance companies work by using codes, with each code corresponding to a specific service. These codes are called *Current Procedural Terminology* (CPT*) codes. Insurance companies must deal with all kinds of medical procedures, and they need a way to standardize them. Each code has units, and those units dictate the amount of service used. For ABA services, units are usually time based. For example, 1 hour of Registered Behavior Technician* (RBT*) time would be four 15-minute units. Things get tricky because different codes have different unit allotments, and those allotments are different depending on the insurance company. As the clinician, you are the one assigning dosage, so it's important that you get familiar with the available codes and how the units work for those codes.

Speaking of codes, once when working with a client who was covered by an insurance company that I was not familiar with, I only requested 15 minutes for an 8-hour reassessment. This happened because some insurance companies use time-based codes (so if you wanted 8 hours, that would be 32 units) and others use a single code for an assessment (meaning 1 unit pays a flat rate for the assessment regardless of how long it takes). The client was not negatively impacted, but I was not our billing department's favorite BCBA that day. It ended up being corrected, but it was a headache for everyone—mostly because no one noticed until they tried to bill for the reassessment—oops!

PRIOR AUTHORIZATIONS

When little Andre's caregivers walk in the door and inquire about services, you need to do an assessment first, right? Not if you want to get paid for doing it. Someone from your company would first do a verification of benefits. This asks the insurance company what the benefit (i.e., rules for payment) is/are for Andre's specific insurance plan. Andre's plan may need a *prior authorization*.

Figure 4.1: *Pursuing a Prior Authorization*

Once you receive the prior authorization, you can begin the assessment process. Several insurance companies have unique requirements for what goes into an assessment. A good rule of thumb is to take the insurance company with the most stringent requirements and make a template. Most ABA companies will have the most senior clinical member make these templates.

STANDARD INSURANCE TEMPLATE SECTIONS

Background:
Who is this person, and how does their history play into their skills and deficits now? A friend of mine was a reviewer for a major insurance company and noted that ABA reports often included unnecessary, unflattering language. Take a look at the two examples below.

- Example 1: "Sam is an athletic and affectionate 4-year-old with a diagnosis of autism spectrum disorder. His current communication modality is pointing and gesturing. He does not utilize vocal-verbal behavior; this is a priority for caregivers."

- Example 2: "Sam is a nonverbal child with autism spectrum disorder. He is 4 years old. His mother wants him to speak like other children his age."

Example 1 presents the same facts as Example 2, but Example 1 focuses on the whole child and how he communicates, instead of only addressing the diagnosis and skill deficits.

At the time of my training, we were taught to use person-first language; it was considered best practice. Now there is more discussion about person-first versus identity-first language. The broad strokes are that some individuals prefer person first as they feel their diagnoses are only a portion of their overall identity. Other individuals prefer identity first because they feel that their diagnosis is an integral part of their identity. My intention is not to oversimplify a complicated issue, and you can and should continue to follow these discussions as they relate to the communities and populations you serve. Instead of trying to use a blanket application of person-first or identify-first language, focus on making sure your documentation is reflective and respectful of each client and how they view themselves (Woolridge, 2023).

Assessments:

What tools did you use to benchmark the deficits of the client? You do not need to prove any diagnosis, but you do need to document that what you plan to do is needed. There are certain assessments that are preferred by insurance companies. In general, here are a few things to remember:

1. You do not need to choose only one.

2. A strong assessment section objectively demonstrates baseline (for initial assessments) and client growth (for reassessments).

3. If you were using one assessment in your first treatment plan and you change your mind for the reassessment, you should still run the first one for an apples-to-apples comparison.

4. You do not need to make magic. If the progress is not demonstrated in the assessments, discuss why.

   • "The individual benchmarks in the domain of 'x' on the 'y' assessment do not best capture the growth of the client."

Plan of Care:

Now that you have established room for growth, what are you going to do about it? What skills will you build, and what behavioral excesses will you need to remediate? How will you maintain these gains? Your goals should be attainable, measurable, meaningful, and related to the deficits you found in the assessment portion.

On my very first plan of care, I wrote 30-something goals for a child receiving a moderate amount of therapy in proportion to his skill deficits and behavior excesses. For some reason, I was under the impression that I needed to try to work on all the deficits at once. At this point, I was doing all my own direct service (meaning I was the one implementing programs), and the progress monitoring alone made me want to rip out my hair.

When it was time to update the assessment 6 months later, I turned to my mentor at the time and said, "Why did you let me do this?" In reality, I'm not even sure I showed her the plan—my statement was in exasperation with myself, not her. I distinctly remember her drinking from a giant, personalized coffee cup as she said, "So you'd never do it again."

The learning opportunity was a great one, and I didn't make that mistake again thanks to her.

Recommendations:

How much time do you need to meet the goals you set? Consider how much you need of the following: supervision, RBT hours, and caregiver training.

Where I ran into trouble in the beginning was that I was used to doing all the direct service/program implementation for my clients. Insurance used to pay for that back in the day, so it wasn't uncommon to see a BCBA in the role that we now primarily see RBTs in. This skewed what I thought was an appropriate dosage. There are industry standards, and each ABA company and insurance company has its own guidelines. The standards and rules that I use are likely to be obsolete by the time this chapter is finished. That said, you as the provider are the one responsible for making the decisions about dosage. You may come across unethical practices or expectations that require you to request the maximum units available for an insurance plan, regardless of the need demonstrated in the assessment. But know this: No one can require you to request the maximum units available.

When you are thinking about your clinical recommendations, give yourself enough time to get everything done you need to, but remember that intensive ABA is about quality over quantity. I have been on the caregiver end of this as well. My son was prescribed 40 hours of ABA, 4 hours of speech, 2 hours of occupational therapy (OT), and 2 hours of physical therapy (PT) a week. That came to a total of 48 hours of therapy weekly, not including medical appointments or educational needs, and all were only available during the same 40-hour business week. That particular ABA company had a policy that if the family couldn't commit to the recommended therapy hours, they would discharge them after assessment, and that was what ended up happening. The issue wasn't just a math problem but an issue with rigidity and potentially not using treatment time as wisely as possible. As a clinician, you should take care with what and how much you are recommending for each client and consider the plausibility of it all.

INSURANCE DECISIONS AND MOVING FORWARD

Treatment ... Almost

Now that you have submitted your assessment to the insurance company, they will respond to you at any time 3–30 days later. They can *approve, deny, partially deny,* request a *peer-to-peer review,* or *pend* the plan.

- **Approved:** Congratulations, you can treat!

- **Denied:** Each company will have an appeals process. Look at the reason they denied the plan, make the appropriate changes, and follow the appeals process. Be sure to keep the client in the know about what is happening.

- **Partially Denied:** This means that certain aspects of your plan were denied but others were approved. In my experience, I've only had partial denials because I've requested "too much" supervision. You can appeal a partial denial or just move on with the number of units they give you.

- **Peer-to-Peer Review:** Some insurance companies will do this as a standard practice, while others will do this with partial denials. I personally love peer-to-peer reviews. It gives you the opportunity to talk to another practitioner—sometimes a psychologist, BCBA, or nurse—about what the unique needs of the case are. It is important to be cordial and professional on these calls. This is not a war, and they are not your enemy. I like to think of it as improving the plan for the insurance company, which ultimately helps the client.

- **Pend:** This is the one I have had the most experience with. A pend is essentially a delay in approval until you make some changes or provide additional information. Most of the times that I've been pended, the information was in fact present in the report, but it wasn't clear enough, or didn't have its own subheading. Once, I received a pend because it was not clear whether the graphs should be going up or down. I had to write under all my graphs, "an upward trend demonstrates progress." I also received a pend once that asked me to include graphs, but graphs were in the original report. In that instance I just had bad luck with the reviewer, as it has not been an issue again. The trouble with pends is that you have a very short amount of time to respond. If you get a pend, make it a priority to complete it as soon as possible.

Treatment ... Finally!

Now that you have your approved units, you have essentially been handed a pile of tokens. Each company has rules on how you can spend your tokens, but for the most part, it's a big pile that you can divvy up as you see fit. If the client goes out of town and misses some sessions, you have extra tokens in the bank that you can use on days they may be out of school or have more availability. There is some flexibility there, but you don't want to overdo it. Have a clear plan and try to be consistent in your implementation. Utilizing your tokens will impact your ability to be authorized for further treatment.

More Treatment ... Maybe?

The consequence of not using all of your tokens is that in the reassessment (should you request one), the insurance company is likely to say, "Well, you didn't use all your tokens from the last plan, so you clearly don't need that many." There may have been good reasons why you did not use those tokens, and you can explain that in your reassessment. Maybe you just didn't need them to make the progress you set out to make—that would be great news. If something changes and you end up needing more, you can request them, as long as you include the rationale for needing them. That said, it won't be an instant process. In the meantime, if you run out you will not be paid for any services provided.

SURVIVAL BASICS

I wouldn't call insurance a necessary evil—it's pretty neat that families don't always have to pay out of pocket for our life-changing, but expensive, service. It's more like a necessary inconvenience. There are things you can do to make it easier for yourself and your clients.

- Know your codes and how they work. I recommend keeping a cheat sheet.

- Remember you don't need to be a miracle worker—just a thorough communicator.

- Make sure your recommendations are reasonable: enough treatment time for you without being impossible for the family to implement.

- Keep track of the reasons behind any pends or denials you receive. That way you can make adjustments to future plans you submit.

✨ ACTIVITY 4.1: CODE BREAKER

Instructions: We've spent this chapter talking a lot about codes. In the spirit of codes and cracking them, use this cryptograph to decipher one of the most commonly used codes in ABA. *See p. 147 to check your answers.*

Hint: CPT Code 97153

A	B	C	D	E	F	G	H	I	J	K	L	M
24		13	15		2		14	18		16		22

N	O	P	Q	R	S	T	U	V	W	X	Y	Z
9		10		21	5		17		3	1		26

24	15	24	10	12	18	19	25

23	25	14	24	19	18	20	21

12	21	25	24	12	22	25	9	12

23	4		10	21	20	12	20	13	20	6

CHAPTER 5

Document or It Didn't Happen

There are two certainties in ABA: acronyms and documentation. Documentation is critical in our field because of our data-driven nature and status as a healthcare field.

The documentation you will deal with can be roughly lumped into two categories: the everyday (little) documentation and the official (big) documentation. Everyday documentation includes what you do with your time, and official documentation comes less often and is likely to be on time schedules set by others (e.g., treatment plans and evaluations).

EVERYDAY DOCUMENTATION

What Do You Need to Keep Track of?

Everything. I'm not even kidding. You wish I were kidding. I wish I were kidding, but I'm not. Not to put too fine a point on it, but if you didn't document it, it didn't happen. Anytime you have contact with a client, whether for reimbursable services or just a quick conversation, you need to document it. You will also need to keep track of your data, and session notes, whether that is on paper or digitally. You should frame your documentation around these questions:

- What did you do?
- When did you do it?
- What were the results?
- What other parties were involved?
- What was the other party's response to your actions/statements?
- What will happen next, and who will be responsible for it?

66

Anytime you have contact with a client, whether for reimbursable services or just a quick conversation, you need to document it.

99

Example documentation for a phone call:

> Caregiver contact took place on 1/12/2023. The call was to confirm the schedule update for the week of 1/30/2023. They were receptive to the update and did not request changes. The caregiver reported that the client's speech therapy schedule may change. If the speech therapy schedule changes, it may conflict with the new schedule. A schedule will be emailed on 1/12/2023 by Mariah. Caregiver will confirm speech schedule by 1/15/2023.

I would place that into a contact log I kept in my desk. I would often refer to it to make sure I communicated what I thought I did. Some electronic data collection systems have a virtual contact log feature, which would serve the same purpose.

🎯 EXERCISE 5.1:   CONTACT LOG

Now it's your turn to fill out a contact log for a contact you've made this week. If it's a client contact, please do not include any identifying information.

_____

_____

_____

_____

How Long Do You Need to Keep Track of It?

At the writing of this chapter, medical records need to be kept for 7 years. After that, you can shred it or destroy it (don't just throw it in the trash can if it has personal information!).

When Do You Have to Keep It?

- If it has identifying information on it (e.g., treatment plans, interaction guidelines)
- If it has been used for progress monitoring (e.g., data)

What Do You Do With All That Paper?

Most of the companies I worked for had a central filing system, and these days, electronic medical records are becoming more and more common.

Once, I was working for a company that focused on community-based services. At the time, I was working mostly with adult clients and didn't make it into the central office often. I had a collapsible filing system that I thought worked well. One time I took everything out to restructure it to turn it in to the central office, and I managed to spill an entire 24 oz iced coffee on the pile. I panicked, blew them dry, and turned them in. I like to think that to this day, no one noticed (probably not true).

What I should have done was recopy the data sheets onto new sheets and asked the original data contributors to initial them. The important thing is that the data remain professionally maintained to the best of your ability.

THE BIG STUFF: TREATMENT PLAN

One of the largest pieces of documentation you are going to write will be a *treatment plan*. Treatment planning will likely be the center of your "big" documentation. I use the term treatment plan, but you may also hear plan of care, behavior intervention plan, or behavior support plan. If we get into nuances, each of these are slightly different documents that communicate different information, but what I write here will (hopefully) generalize across all of them.

When Do I Write the Treatment Plan?

Like most things, this will depend on who you are providing services to. In general, when you get a new client, you do an assessment and write the treatment plan. If you are serving an individual who is utilizing insurance reimbursement, you will write an update of this treatment plan every 6 months. If something changes drastically (e.g., new behaviors, you need to request more treatment time) you will need to update portions of the treatment plan prior to these 6-month updates. For adult clients utilizing a waiver service, you may update these documents every year.

How Long Does It Take to Write a Treatment Plan?

When you are first starting out, it may take a while. At the writing of this chapter, the standard insurance payout for a treatment plan is the equivalent of 8 hours (i.e., insurance companies think it will take you 8 hours). It may take you more or less time, but give yourself *at least* 8 hours. I am providing a non-exhaustive list of some of the activities you do as part of an assessment. As you read through these, think about your own strengths and weaknesses and how they may play into timing. For example, I am a quick reader, so the records review is the "shortest" aspect of my assessment. However, I know I will need to make several revisions during the write-up process, so that takes longer.

Treatment Plan Activities

- **Comprehensive records review.** Review items like the intake packet, diagnostic evaluations, IEP, records from previous providers, and any previous treatment plans. This will help you fill in the background information on the client and give you an idea of who the client is. I usually do these reviews prior to meeting with the client whenever possible. I have found it helps me make the most out of face time with the client.

- **Caregiver, stakeholder, and client interview.** In situations where I have a caregiver describing a client, I like to have this conversation away from the client so that everyone can speak freely. I will also interview the client with or without the caregiver present (the questions for the client interview are tailored to their age and communication modality). I will also interview any caregivers in other environments (e.g., teachers, daycare providers), dependent upon having the appropriate HIPAA releases.

- **Observations.** I try to observe the client in all relevant environments (school, daycare, home, in clinic), although you may not have the opportunity or releases to do this.

- **Direct assessments.** I run preference assessments in addition to standardized assessments (VB-MAPP, AFLS) as the client tolerates. If the assessment is the first time that I meet the client, I like to take the opportunity to pair myself with reinforcement. Some of these assessments are long and take several hours to administer. If the client does not tolerate testing and I have to lean heavily on caregiver reports, I will make note of this in the report.

- **Write-up.** It's time to synthesize everything and write it down!

As you start writing these for yourself, keep track of how long the process takes you, so you can better plan for additional assessments as they come up.

What Goes Into a Treatment Plan?

The individual components of a treatment plan will change depending on the payor and the purpose of the document.

Follow along with the fictional treatment plan for an insurance company in Figure 5.1 on the next few pages to get an idea of the process.

Do I Have to Write the Treatment Plan by Myself?

Yes and no. If you are the BCBA for the client, the treatment plan is quite literally your plan for how to treat the client. Each company will have templates for you to use, so you aren't completely on your own. Each payor will also have different requirements, so when in doubt you can check on these requirements. If you inherit a client from another BCBA at your company, you can use their treatment plan until it is time for an update. Even though you ultimately have ownership of the document, almost every section is written in collaboration with someone.

The client's caregivers or the client themself will be providing you with background information (medical and social history) and their priorities for goals. During the assessment/reassessment phase, you will continue to lean on caregiver and client reports, in addition to your own observations and data.

While conducting an assessment (like the VB-MAPP or ABLLS-R), you may have an assistant supporting you in doing the assessment. This isn't always common practice, so don't feel slighted if that isn't available to you. When it comes to scoring the assessment, there are scoring guides to help you. These guides are very detailed and often include what to do if your client only demonstrates portions of the skill in that benchmarking category. With standardized assessments, there are examples of how to display this information.

Figure 5.1: *Treatment Plan Walk-Through*

Behavior Assessment and Plan of Care

Recipient's Name: Nota Realperson

Recipient's DOB: 01/01/2020

Recipient's Age: This is redundant I know, but sometimes it's a payor requirement, and I like the fact that it saves the reader some mental math.

Evaluator's Name: This is you.

Date of Report: Include the dates of the assessments.

Learner Profile

The learner profile is also sometimes called the background; both will work just fine. The purpose of this is to provide a detailed snapshot of the individual. Recall our discussion on person-first and identify-first language in Chapter 4, and remember to speak to who they are and not just provide a listing of their diagnosis and deficits. The first sentence or so should be an introduction of the individual.

Don't do:

Nota has autism spectrum disorder. Her mother and grandmother are concerned that she has not developed like, and cannot communicate like, her peers.

Why could this example use improvement? Because although communicating a diagnosis is very important to any potential payors, this is the first thing someone is going to learn about Nota, and we should show her as a whole person.

Try this:

Nota is an affectionate and athletically inclined 4-year-old girl who lives at home with her mother and grandmother. Nota was diagnosed with autism spectrum disorder by Dr. Iam Adoctor on 06/01/2022.

Why is this example better? It provides more detailed and concise information, while saying more about who Nota is as a person. We want the person reading this to have a snapshot of who Nota is. what skills she has, and what supports she needs. We are trying to represent as much of Nota in that moment as we can.

Other information to consider including in this section:

- Comorbid conditions (other diagnoses outside of the primary diagnosis that brought them in to see you; includes allergies)
- Any medications they take
- If information on gestation and delivery is available and relevant, provide that
- Any notable childhood injuries, hospitalizations, or other relevant medical history

- Any relevant family history or circumstances that may impact how you deliver treatment
- If the person is receiving any other services or ongoing medical treatment
- Any relevant dietary restrictions
- Any disrupted or alternative sleep schedules
- Specific concerns brought up by the individual or their caregiver

For example:

Nota is reported to be within standard deviation for her motor milestones. Her mother reported that although she can physically perform these tasks, her ability to follow directions and lack of impulse control put her and others at risk when she completes physical activity. Her mother brought up an example of an adapted gymnastics lesson in which Nota did not follow directions to remain in the area and encountered another child who was tumbling. Neither party was seriously injured, but the potential for injury was high. Nota's mother, Ms. Realperson, reports concern that Nota is not able to communicate her injuries and worries for Nota's well-being after incidents such as this.

Caregiver Interview (or Interview With the Individual)

In this section, summarize the interview you did as a part of the assessment. If you did multiple interviews (e.g., teacher, babysitter, and caregiver; for an adult client: each shift of caregivers), you could combine them, but I like to keep them in separate subsections for clarity.

Observation in Environment

In this section, summarize the observation you did as a part of the assessment. Keep things as matter of fact as possible. Did the client respond to instructions? How did the teacher describe them? How did they interact with their peers? It is ideal to make multiple observations across environments.

Assessments Results With Client Abilities and Needs

I like to list out the assessment(s) and scores first, and then place a rendering of the grid. Below that I will break down the assessment by individual domains and write as plainly as possible what that means. I personally like to use multiple assessments, one as a primary and others to flesh out any deficits. For example, if Listener Responding is a lower scoring developmental domain, I may pull in that section of the ABLLS-R.

VB-MAPP

Scores and grid could go here.

Here is an example breakdown using the VB-MAPP (Sundberg, 2014).

Results from VB-MAPP assessment

> **Listener Responding by Function, Feature, and Class:**
> This domain assesses **receptive language skills**, such as following complex instructions and demonstrating discrimination by selecting items by function, feature, and class.

Initial Assessment: 09/01/22 Nota was able to engage in some, but not all, demands in this domain. She was successful in one-step directions (e.g., come here, sit down, let's jump). She has not yet demonstrated the ability to follow multistep directions. She was able to identify objects by name. She is not yet able to identify objects by feature, function, or class. This is consistent with the report from her preschool teacher. It should be noted that not all of Nota's skills may have been demonstrated during the assessment process and additional testing will take place in ongoing treatment. Scores could go here.

Type of Preference Assessment Used (check all that apply)

Please put conscious effort into assessing the preferences of your client. I usually do a caregiver-style interview alongside a more direct preference assessment. Not only will this help in the initial pairing days, but it will also help the reader have a rough idea of things that Nota Realperson has recently liked. Preferences often change, and this will not represent anything "permanent."

☐ Paired-Stimulus Preference Assessment: Number of Items Assessed:

☐ Single-Stimulus Preference Assessment: Duration of Assessment:

☐ Free Operant Observation: Duration of Observation:

☒ Multiple-Stimulus With Replacement: Number of Items Assessed: **30**

☐ Multiple-Stimulus Without Replacement: Number of Items Assessed:

List top 5 items in order of preference

1. Squishy sensory ball filled with rice

2. Stacking silicone blocks (with interlocking ridges)

3. Trains (wooden trains without electronic components)

4. Wooden multi-shape blocks (box of 120)

5. Robot dog (Nota would change the settings of the toy rapidly to create unique sounds)

I also include graphed preference assessments to show if the client participated well and if there was a clear hierarchy. If the client was not interested or refused to participate, you can document that here. Please note how descriptive I was. If anyone else were to use this information, I would want them to know what specific things Nota Realperson likes. Descriptions like "ball" are less helpful because it could be any kind of ball.

Plan of Care

Goals go here. You should match your goals to the needs of the client and the environment. You should demonstrate the need for the goals in the assessment section, but there is no need to use the specific skills listed in the assessment as your goals.

In the example above, I demonstrated that Nota Realperson cannot identify objects by feature/function/class or follow multistep directions. Depending on what her needs are, I may choose to target one or both of these areas. If I choose to target these, I will focus on what her needs are in the environment and **not** copy and paste the next VB-MAPP skill.

When writing goals, don't be discouraged if you get "stuck." This is a great thing to collaborate on with a senior BCBA, should you have access to one. If you don't have access to a collaborator, here are some questions to go through as a thought exercise.

- Who does this goal benefit? *If the client isn't the first person on the list of beneficiaries, then reconsider the goal.*
- What skills will this goal "open up"? *This question can help you narrow down goals that will have more potential impact.*
- What environments will these goals open up, if any?
- Do these goals impact the client's ability to communicate/have influence over their environment? *Remember that you should focus on empowering the client to have their wants and needs met and not focus too much on compliance.*

ABA Principles and Interventions That Will Be Used

What techniques or environmental modifications are you recommending?

For Nota Realperson:

- Differential reinforcement
- Errorless teaching
- Intensive teaching/discrete trial teaching
- Natural environment teaching
- Prompting and prompt fading
- Chaining
- Shaping
- Modeling
- Positive reinforcement

Skill Generalization

This was a section that was required by some payors at the writing of this chapter. Here is a non-exhaustive example for Nota.

The following strategies will be utilized to promote generalization.

- Use of multiple exemplars: using a variety of stimuli and response outcomes
- Novel retention checks
- General case analysis: identifying and selecting teaching examples that represent the full range of stimulus variations and response requirements in the generalization setting
- Programming common stimuli: using the generalized and natural setting in the teaching environment
- Training across multiple instructors: use of 2–3 Registered Behavior Technicians
- Training across novel settings: transferring skills/behaviors learned under one set of circumstances, such as the teaching setting, to other situations
- Choosing behaviors that will contact reinforcement in the natural environment: selecting behaviors that will contact reinforcement to increase appropriate responding directly related to play or daily routines
- Daily maintenance checks: providing opportunities to demonstrate previously acquired skills over time and over durations in which the reinforcement has been thinned below the level at which the skill was taught in the first place
- Teaching loosely: varying the environment within the teaching setting to encourage generalization; varying the time of day, temperature, teacher, choice of words, etc.; being as unpredictable and random as possible to encourage the learning to happen across settings
- Caregiver training: practicing and training targeted skills across environments and people
- Coordination of care across providers: sharing treatment plan with other professionals providing services to the learner; contacting providers via email or phone to share programming information that can be beneficial to them; and requesting information from other providers that can be beneficial to ABA treatment

Risks Associated With Treatment Include

For Nota Realperson:

- Temporary increase in the frequency, duration, and magnitude of behaviors targeted for reduction

Risks Associated With Withholding Treatment Include

For Nota Realperson:

- Continued use of maladaptive behavior to gain access to preferred items; as Nota Realperson matures, aggressive behaviors (hitting) may present a danger to family members

Service Recommendations Based on Assessed Needs of Beneficiary

This is where you put your hours recommendations.

Schedule of Therapy

Some payors require this. It usually looks something like this:

Monday–Friday 9:00 a.m.–12:00 p.m.

Coordination of Care

In this section, you describe how you will work with the child's caregivers and other service providers. Sometimes you will note here that a copy of the report will be sent to the pediatrician upon caregiver request. Individual payors have specific requirements.

Discharge Plan

In this section, you describe under what conditions the client will be ready for discharge. This section may have a fading plan, meaning how you intend to get them from full schedule to discharge.

Crisis Plan

Does your client engage in any crisis behavior? You may need to create a crisis plan. Some payors require this section regardless. Nota Realperson's insurance required this section, so I put in one like this.

Please note risk factors:

- ☐ Assaultive behavior
- ☐ Impulsive behavior
- ☐ Elopement
- ☐ Psychotic symptoms
- ☒ Other: none

- ☐ Self-injurious behavior (SIB)
- ☐ Self-mutilation/cutting
- ☐ Sexually offending behavior
- ☐ Coping with significant loss (job, relationship, financial)

- ☐ Fire setting
- ☐ Current family violence
- ☐ Current substance abuse

Nota Realperson will be referred to a more appropriate provider if she cannot be safely treated at the current level of care. It is not expected for that to be the case.

Please contact me if you have any questions about this plan. I can be reached at: (add email and phone number)

_____

BCBA/Date

My signature indicates that I was involved in the process of the Individual Plan of Care (IPOC) and was offered a copy.

_____

Caregiver Signature/Date

Choosing goals is perhaps the most subjective aspect of the treatment plan. You may find tools online along the lines of "recommended goals for 'x' assessment." These can serve as inspiration, but I encourage you to consider the needs of the individual as you write goals. Asking to read treatment plans written by other BCBAs can be helpful to understand how to write your own, but resist the urge to copy and paste. It can also be helpful to think back on your time gathering fieldwork hours—what were the goals you worked on with clients under the direction of your supervisor? How were they structured? What did you like and not like about them?

Once you have written the treatment plan, most organizations will have a senior BCBA who can review your treatment plan as part of a standardized process. This usually includes reviewing the appropriateness of your goals and dosage.

If you find yourself needing assistance to complete the report, you certainly aren't alone. Reach out to another BCBA at your company (anyone *outside* of your company would require a HIPAA release). Try to be specific when you ask for help. Instead of saying, "I don't know how to do this," ask something like, "My client shows skill deficits in receptive identification; what kind of goal should I write to address this?" or "Could you please review my background section? I'm not sure I have captured all relevant information." There are also continuing education units (CEUs) about writing better behavior plans and treatment plans that you could add to your continuing education plan. See more on CEUs in Chapter 11.

A treatment plan is likely going to be one of the largest single pieces of documentation you write as a behavior analyst. Best practices will continue to evolve (you may never write one that looks like the example above) and it's important to remain flexible as you continue in your career.

SURVIVAL BASICS

Documentation Quick Tips and Takeaways:

- Follow up phone conversations and meetings with written communication with the party that includes the action items and issues that were addressed.
- Write texts/emails like they will be read out loud in court someday.
- Never leave sensitive information in your car.
- Don't drink giant iced coffees while working with paper data (this one may be just for me).
- Learn your organization's rules and regulations around documentation.
- Identify individuals in your organization who can provide peer reviews of your documentation.
- Take extra care when completing official documentation.

CHAPTER 6

Communication, Corrective Feedback, and Conflict

COMMUNICATION

As a clinical BCBA, I spent most of my time talking, but that doesn't mean I was a good communicator. Communication at its core is being able to convey information clearly and wholly, in a way that gets things done. Being a good communicator includes being able to navigate conflict and being able to give and receive corrective feedback. These are all things I had to learn through trial and error; a mix of "well that worked" and "oh no, that was a disaster." This chapter includes everything I learned along the way.

Active Listening

Communication starts with listening. The goal is twofold: You need to aim to fully understand what is being said, implicitly and explicitly, while communicating to the other person your interest and engagement (Abrahams & Groysberg, 2021). We can further divide this into three parts:

1. Cognitive (It feels like a dirty word in a behavior-analytic text, I know.)

    *   This part of active listening focuses on understanding what is being communicated to you. Focus on receiving what is being communicated without judgment. Allow the person to fully communicate without argument or interruption. You will have the opportunity to disagree when you aren't listening.

2. Emotional

    *   Beyond just staying calm, manage any emotions you may be feeling. For me, even when I'm not upset, I can sometimes be chomping at the bit for the other person

to finish their thought so I can jump in. This is something that I practice managing during active listening.

3. Behavioral (Technically, it's all behavioral, right? I get it—feel free to rename these.)

  • This part is about communicating to the other person that you are listening. This can be through body language (leaning forward, nodding) or verbal through validating statements (mm-hmm, okay, I hear you, I understand).

Empathy

Empathy in the workplace promotes open communication. If people feel understood—or that others are genuinely attempting to understand them—the motivation to lie no longer exists. Mistakes shouldn't be the signal for punishment. You now work in human services: Empathy is a vital tool for you to connect with your clients, and their caregivers if applicable.

In my career, the client feedback I am most proud of was a caregiver saying, "The best thing about you is that I can be honest. I can tell you our struggles without you thinking I'm just a bad parent or that I don't love my child."

Now, empathy is one of those things that has a connotation of being an inherent trait or part of someone's personality—you either have it or you don't. Empathy is actually a skill that can be cultivated and developed.

⊚ EXERCISE 6.1: EMPATHY PRACTICE

Grab a trusted practice partner and try the following exercises to strengthen your empathy.

1. Perception and Detection:

  Do an activity with your partner like grabbing a cup of coffee. Summarize the emotions you sense and the words you hear from your practice partner as you have a typical inter-action, and let them respond with agreement or corrections.

  a. Your example summary: "Your arms were crossed when you said the coffee shop was closed. I am sensing that you are angry."

  b. Your partner's example response: "No, I am just exhausted and really wanted that coffee. I'm more disappointed than anything."

  c. What was your experience with this exercise? Did it go as you expected, or were there some surprises?

2. Story Interrupted:

   Provide your partner with a few topics to share stories about with you—particularly some that are likely to remind you of stories you would like to share. Practice listening without sharing or interrupting. Once you start planning the story you want to tell, you aren't listening anymore.

   a. How long did you last before you started planning your own story?

   b. How long did you last before interrupting? *When I tried out this activity, my practice partner actively tried to get me to interrupt, which made it fun. I lasted 6 minutes and ultimately interrupted to explain the difference between alpacas and llamas.*

3. Looking Glass:

   We all have lenses through which we see the world. These lenses can impact how we interpret information. For example, as a social media user and active coffee consumer, I read a section of a report out loud to my colleague that said, "X communicates using PSL," and automatically read it as "pumpkin spice latte" instead of the intended message of "Pakistan Sign Language." These lenses could be a protected status (age, orientation, gender identity) or another aspect of your identity (craftsperson, behavior analyst, animal lover). Discuss your lenses with your partner.

   a. How could your differences impact the way you interpret the same information?

4. Complicit Complaining:

   Provide your partner with a few topics to complain about with you—again preferably topics that you also have complaints about. Don't jump in and agree with them. Practice getting to the root of the problem through redirecting. Practice giving sympathetic statements without confirming or denying the accuracy of what your partner is saying.

   a. What was your experience with this exercise? Was the redirection effective?

Keeping your communication empathetic is an important skill that will likely spill over into conflict resolution. Everyone wants to be seen and heard when they are expressing themselves.

Preferences

Keep in mind that different individuals have unique communication preferences. Understanding these will help ensure that your contacts with them start off on the right foot. My personal preferences for work communications are: (a) text for urgent but not emergent; (b) "ICE (in case of emergency), call twice" so I know to step away regardless of what I'm doing; and (c) everything else should be email.

🎯 EXERCISE 6.2: YOUR COMMUNICATION PREFERENCES

Take a moment to think about what your preferences are and jot them down. This will help you think about and be mindful of others' preferences.

- When should you be emailed?

- When should you be called?

- When should you be texted or instant messaged?

- What is best to wait to communicate until the next point of contact (e.g., next supervision or caregiver training)?

FEEDBACK OR CRITICISM?

"Feedback" can sometimes be used interchangeably with "criticism." I've been in several environments where feedback was a euphemism for getting my you-know-what handed to me on a platter. As a result of this learned history, I anxiously observed the moods of my superiors. I was sensitive to even the best delivered feedback. Worst of all, I didn't have the skill of giving feedback. It took time and self-work to deprogram and reprogram my behavior around feedback.

🎯 EXERCISE 6.3: FEEDBACK REFLECTION

Even though you are likely just starting out your career as a behavior analyst, this won't be the first time you receive or give feedback. We bring our learned history with us to work, so think about how yours may be impacting how you give and receive feedback.

I most often receive feedback that is: (check all that apply)

☐ critical

☐ positive

☐ supportive

☐ calm

☐ given when the speaker is angry

☐ reciprocal

☐ verbal

☐ in writing

My first memory of receiving professional feedback is:

_____

_____

_____

I believe my initial experiences with professional feedback impact the way I receive feedback by:

_____

_____

_____

Learning to Offer Corrective Feedback

As a behavior analyst, you are now in a position to offer *corrective feedback* to those in supporting roles. This may be the first time you are in that position—it certainly was for me. When I was first starting, my support team was the same group that had been my peer group just 4 months prior. I opted to just not give feedback, which limited conflict but ultimately wasn't the best option.

When offering corrective feedback, you should:

- **Be mindful of your emotional state.** If you're feeling upset about something (even if it's their mistake), try to check your temper or tone. Coming across as angry won't change the situation, except to make it worse by hurting your relationship with your support team or peer. No one needs to be scolded.

- **Be confident about what your goal is.** If your goal is to "vent" or express frustration, the feedback is better left unsaid.

- **Be aware of your relationship with the person.** We are often "harsher" on those with whom we have a closer relationship. On the other hand, you may not know the person or situation well enough to offer feedback.

- **Be specific.** It is not enough to say, "Good job" or "Try again." For feedback to be effective, it must be as specific as possible.

- **Give feedback on things under the performer's control.** Make sure that the performance is something that is actually under the performer's control. I've gotten frustrated with an RBT for not running programs when it turns out the stimuli that were needed were in my car.

- **Give feedback immediately.** The closer the feedback is to the performance, the more effective it will be. The concepts that apply to clients apply to us.

Receiving Feedback

When receiving feedback, do not outwardly disagree in the moment. If you disagree with the feedback, there will be an opportunity to regroup and discuss that. Ask for

> *If your goal is to "vent" or express frustration, the feedback is better left unsaid.*

clarification if you don't understand the feedback. Nodding and maintaining open body language will go a long way. It's important to understand that giving feedback can be as uncomfortable as receiving it.

If you find yourself sensitive to feedback, practice reaffirming phrases like: "I can use this feedback to improve myself" and "Learning is continuous."

🔘 EXERCISE 6.4: FEEDBACK AFFIRMATIONS

Write your own affirmations here:

CONFLICT RESOLUTION

Conflict resolution is essential to maintaining a productive workforce and high workplace morale. In the high-stress world of ABA, I highly doubt you will be able to survive without experiencing some conflict. There are different types of conflict. As you experience conflict, try to categorize it (Herrity, 2022):

- **intrapersonal conflict:** within one person
- **interpersonal conflict:** between two or more people
- **intergroup conflict:** between groups of people

1. Understand the conflict

    - Before you begin communicating your way through a conflict, make sure you understand your position and the position of the other person/people. What are your motivations and actions and what are theirs? Try to keep this as behavior-analytic as possible and try not to fall into the pitfalls of all-or-nothing thinking. Think about what it is that you really care about in the conflict, what your concerns are, and what you would like to see happen (Herrity, 2022).

☀️ TOOL 6.1:   WORKING THROUGH CONFLICT

Instructions: Below is a series of questions to help you understand the conflict. Respond to each question for all parties involved in the conflict. Once you have completed the questions for each party, use the final prompts to find common ground.

Party 1's Perspective (the conflict party that does not include you)	**Party 2's Perspective** (the conflict party that includes you)	**Party 3's Perspective** (optional, the other conflict party that does not include you)
• What started the conflict?	• What started the conflict?	• What started the conflict?
• How has the conflict made them feel?	• How has the conflict made you feel?	• How has the conflict made them feel?
• What actions have they taken to resolve the conflict?	• What actions have you taken to resolve the conflict?	• What actions have they taken to resolve the conflict?
• What outcome would be ideal?	• What outcome would be ideal?	• What outcome would be ideal?
• What outcome would be acceptable?	• What outcome would be acceptable?	• What outcome would be acceptable?
• What outcome would be unacceptable?	• What outcome would be unacceptable?	• What outcome would be unacceptable?

What do all perspectives have in common?

What outcomes are acceptable to all parties?

2. Explore alternatives and boundaries

- In some cases, the parties are not able to reach an agreeable solution in a conflict. Think about what compromises you can make in the moment and when you will need to regroup. Oftentimes, conflicts don't require an immediate solution.

3. Navigate the conflict conversation

- It's not a win/lose game

    o If you walk into a conflict resolution meeting with the attitude that you're going to win, then no one will. Remind yourself of what the goal is. I do this by placing a sticky note discreetly on my desk with one word on it that relates to the goal.

- Clarify, clarify, clarify

    o Chances are both parties are walking into a negotiation with a lot of preconceived ideas of what the other wants. Now that you are a behavior analyst, use the same skill set you use to create operational definitions to create clear objectives for the conversation (Schindler, 2019).

- Find a private, neutral place

    o It's important to find a quiet and neutral location where you can discuss conflict in private. An office or conference room works well if you can close the doors and speak privately without being interrupted. That said, some conflicts require a neutral witness, like a human resources (HR) representative or a manager, so defer to your company's policy and best practices.

- Have open body language

    o Body language is a large part of how we communicate. How you are perceived is impacted by how you present that information.

        - Practice giving positive and corrective feedback in a mirror.

            • Which one felt more natural?

            • How does your facial expression change between the positive and corrective feedback?

        - Get back together with your practice partner and video-record you two role-playing a difficult conversation.

            • The first time, play it back as *audio* only.

- How did your tone communicate your intent?

- Were your words clear?
    - The second time, play it back as *video* only.
        - Did your body language match your words?
        - What did your body language say about the conflict that your words did not?

4. Find a common goal
   - When you communicate with the other party or parties in the conflict, establish what your goal is and what you have in common. Focusing on the elements you share will help keep the conversation productive.

5. Brainstorm solutions
   - Try to come up with as many ideas as possible. Look for win-win solutions or compromises that all parties can agree upon.
   - Discuss each idea. Do not outright discount the solutions presented by the other party. Consider the pros and cons of each solution, as well as what it would take to implement that solution. If an idea cannot be used, discuss why it won't work. That way all parties are heard. *See Tool 6.2.*

6. Make a plan of action
   - Once you have found one or more solutions, draft out the next steps. Assign who will complete what next steps. Finalize this in writing to maintain accountability on all sides. *See Tool 6.3.*

☀ TOOL 6.2: CONFLICT SOLUTIONS

Instructions: On the next page is a grid you can use to help with these solutions. Fill out the solution (note that there is nowhere to write whose solution it is), the short- and long-term pros and cons, and the action items needed from each party. If you aren't familiar with an action item, it's something that needs to be done in order to accomplish something. So, in this case, it would be something that needs to be done for the solution to be viable. I also left a space for you to rank the potential solutions.

Conflict Solutions

Solution	Short-term PROS	Short-term CONS	Long-term PROS	Long-term CONS	Action items needed to implement	Action items for Party 1	Action items for Party 2	Notes	Rank the solutions

☀ TOOL 6.3:   CONFLICT ACTION PLANNING

Instructions: On the next page is a project planning sheet you can use to help with conflict solutions and plans of action. Fill out the action items, who is responsible, the tentative completion date, and any notes. I like to color-code the status bar—color in each status box according to the legend below (examples in parentheses):

- ☐ Completed (blue)
- ☐ In Process (green)
- ☐ At Risk (yellow)
- ☐ Behind (red)
- ☐ Not Started (gray)

SURVIVAL BASICS

Communication, corrective feedback, and conflict resolution are things that will continue to come up in your professional career. Although the tools here are definitely meant to help you survive, circle back to them again once you are out of survival mode and see how they feel.

Conflict Action Planning

Project Activity	Responsible Party	Tentative Completion Date	Status	Notes

CHAPTER 7

Taking on Imposter Syndrome

Being a behavior analyst, you will have some losses, but you will also have great wins. I can vividly remember the first time I had a successful echoic with a client and when I taught someone to respond to and write their name.

While I rode the high that came from moments like those, there was a little voice in my head finding qualifiers for them, like "It was luck." Several other new BCBAs at my first job also had that little voice; it was something that brought us all together. That same little voice can pop up when you have to do something new or scary: "You can't do this," "You aren't qualified."

That little voice has a lot of names, but the one I'll be using is *imposter syndrome*. You won't find any of its names in the *DSM* (at least at the writing of this chapter), and it isn't considered a disorder. The first article on imposter syndrome was written by Georgia State University psychologists Pauline Rose Clance and Suzanne Imes in 1978. It described "impostor phenomenon" as the term used "to designate an internal experience of intellectual phoniness" (p. 241). I recommend giving it a read when you have a chance.

See Activity 7.1 on the following page.

If you have managed to get bingo, you may have imposter syndrome. I say this in a tongue-in-cheek way, of course, as bingo is not a recognized self-assessment tool. If you want an actual self-assessment tool, I recommend the Clance Impostor Phenomenon Scale (CIPS) (Clance, 1985). Currently, whether some groups are more likely to be impacted than others is up for debate, with research on either side. All things considered, it's safe to say: If you feel this way, you are not alone.

✨ ACTIVITY 7.1: IMPOSTER SYNDROME BINGO

Instructions: Put an "X" on squares that sound like you, and see if you get bingo!

B	I	N	G	O
Using negative self-talk, even after "wins" and "good days"	Fearing you'll be "found out"	Discounting success (it's no big deal)	Lacking confidence in your position	Attributing success to others' faulty judgment
Attributing success to luck	Constantly comparing yourself to other people	Feeling like you have used charm to get where you are	Working extra hard to avoid being "found out"	Having difficulty taking ownership of your success
Assuming no one else makes the same mistakes as you	Attributing success to high effort only	FREE SPACE	Feeling like a fake	Apologizing for every small flaw
Feeling like if you're not a genius, you're unintelligent	Being sensitive to even the best presented constructive criticism	Attributing success to accidents	Avoiding promotion seeking because you don't feel like you "deserve" it	Feeling as though you don't deserve recognition
Believing people are nice to you out of pity	Feeling like you have been overestimated	Having low expectations for your success	Dwelling on mistakes	Being full of self-doubt

(Clance & Imes, 1978)

IMPOSTER SYNDROME CAN LOOK LIKE ...

In her book *The Secret Thoughts of Successful Women* (2023), Dr. Valerie Young details five different ways imposter syndrome can manifest. I've taken liberties in the presentation, but these manifestations belong to her. The manifestations have positive attributes, but they need to be balanced out to help a person feel less like an imposter.

THE PERFECTIONIST	THE NATURAL GENIUS	THE SOLOIST

Traits:

- If there is a right way and a wrong way to do something, the perfectionist is the only one who knows the right way (aka their way).

- It must be done perfectly or not at all.

- Has a harsh inner critic that drives them.

Traits:

- Wants to go from new-to-this to best-at-this in 0 seconds flat.

- Tends to believe in "talent" and "natural ability."

- Believes in a fixed mindset of skills instead of growth (e.g., if I am not good at it now, I will never be).

Traits:

- Believes true achievement is accomplished alone.

- Would never ask for directions if they missed their exit.

- Has a skewed sense of how much someone can accomplish.

Is balanced by ...

- Determining what the "good enough" standards are for any project.

- Having a trusted mentor to tell them when their perfectionism is hurting progress more than it is helping in quality control.

Is balanced by ...

- Understanding that "talent" or "natural ability" is not a requirement for success.

- Understanding that growth takes effort over time.

Is balanced by ...

- Knowing what resources (including extra hands or more time) you need to complete a project is an important skill.

- Understanding it's okay to build on the resources of others and collaborate.

Figure 7.1: Imposter Syndrome Manifestations (Adapted from Young [2023])

THE EXPERT

THE SUPERHUMAN

Traits

- Incredibly concerned with how much skill and knowledge they have (and they usually have a lot of both).

- Believes that to be an expert, you need to possess all possible knowledge about a specific area.

- Understands their own limitations and is not likely to practice outside of their scope.

Is balanced by ...

- Knowing that an expert doesn't know everything; they know how to find it out.

- Cultivating confidence in the knowledge and skills currently possessed.

Traits

- Has the compulsion to be everything for everyone (the have-it-all mentality).

- Can't seem to say no to any responsibilities.

- Feels guilty for not being able to take on more.

Is balanced by ...

- Understanding that competence does not equal how many things you can do.

- Thinking of delegating as sharing opportunities.

- Remembering that others are watching.**

**I once had a small cohort of graduate students, and I was pulled aside by one. She said, "You know, I don't think I want to be a BCBA anymore. Maybe I will stay an RBT." While I validated that being an RBT is an important and valued role on the team, I asked what brought the change. She said that watching me come in early and stay late every night "doing everything" made her realize that it wasn't worth the stress. At the time, I told her that I did that because *I wasn't efficient enough, and it was my own fault.* It's important to communicate that I truly believed this. I had internalized a toxic work environment and thought if I were just a better BCBA, I wouldn't have to work this hard. I told her I would never expect her to work outside of hours or take work home. It was my job to support her and make sure that didn't happen, at least while I was her team lead. She ended up staying with the program and becoming a BCBA, but I think about that conversation a lot. I wasn't working early/late because I was ineffective or inefficient. I was doing that because I was one of two BCBAs in a very large region (for that company) and oversaw more things than was appropriate by any measure. It took me a few years to stop criticizing my speed of work out loud, but it is still a frequent thought. Now when those thoughts cross my mind, I try to speak to myself the same way I would speak to a new BCBA.

✍ ACTIVITY 7.2:
MY IMPOSTER SYNDROME MANIFESTATION

Instructions: Keeping the above manifestations in mind, which traits most resonate with you? Fill out the boxes below for you to reflect on. This may help you see yourself from a different perspective.

Character name:

My traits:

Sketch your character below:

I will keep these in check by:

GENERAL TIPS

If there were a magic wand to take away any feelings of inadequacy, I would have waved it for you—or at least included it in an appendix. Here's the next best thing I can offer:

Now when those thoughts cross my mind, I try to speak to myself the same way I would speak to a new BCBA.

- You can say "no" without feeling guilty.
  - Practice politely declining a work opportunity.
    - Example: While I would love this experience, it would require more travel than my current schedule allows. If my current schedule and responsibilities can be adjusted to accommodate this new opportunity, that would be ideal. If not, I would unfortunately need to decline.
    - Your turn:

- You don't have to know all the answers.
  - Practice your I-have-no-idea-but-I-need-to-save-face-in-this-moment phrases.
    - Example: I have some ideas, but I'd like to confer with my colleagues. Let's circle back at our next visit, and I will have some options to discuss.
    - Your turn:

- You have the right to a learning curve.
  - Our industry is known for being high stakes and high stress. Every day, I hear more stories of new graduates who are instantly handed caseloads or expected to run facilities. Practice your I'm-just-learning-this-you-can't-leave-me-here-by-myself phrases.
    - Example: Thank you for this opportunity. Given my limited experience in this area, how might I gain experience and feedback from a more senior team member while in this role?

- Your turn:

- You have the right to be heard.
  - If you must continue to fight to be heard, you may be in the wrong room.
  - In one of my early jobs, I was told not to speak in meetings—that I hadn't earned the right to do that. Now to be fair, I had some ideas of grandeur back then, but instead of taking me down a peg, that comment completely deflated me. I internalized this and often found that I had nothing "valuable" to contribute. Practice your I-have-value-to-add affirmations.
    - Example: My perspective is unique, not *despite*, but *because* of my inexperience.
    - Your turn:

SURVIVAL BASICS

As you continue to progress through your early career, continue to give yourself the space to not know all the answers, have a learning curve, and say "no" without feeling guilty. Embrace yourself (and by extension, others) as humans, not superheroes.

CHAPTER 8

Bedside Balance

You're probably familiar with the term "bedside manner." In this chapter, I will avoid using that term because I think it can sometimes be interpreted as synonymous with having good manners or being polite. Obviously, you shouldn't be rude—that is the base expectation. And as a behavior analyst, you are in a position *not to be rude* in a variety of circumstances, including but not limited to:

- Someone actively being physically or verbally aggressive towards themself or others.
- Someone engaging in property destruction.
- Someone saying your viewpoint is wrong from a philosophical perspective.
- Being told you are bribing a child and that's why ABA never works, while actively trying not to get whacked with toy cars flying through the air.
  - That one was a little specific, but you get the idea.

On top of maintaining a professional demeanor during all client or client-related interactions, you also need to be an effective communicator with *bedside balance*.

I define bedside balance as making the space for collaboration and informed consent in your client/caregiver/stakeholder interactions. Note that, in the interest of conciseness, I will use "client" throughout this chapter as an all-inclusive term for "client/caregiver/stakeholder."

SIT DOWN

As a behavior analyst, you are probably "go, go, go" from the start of your day to the end, but don't let that rushing show in your interactions with clients. When you are reviewing, training, or addressing a concern, sit down (metaphorically and literally). Be prepared to stay for a reasonable amount of time (i.e., more than a "quick chat"). When you are connecting with a client, that is the most important thing you could be doing in that moment (assuming no one is injured or in danger).

USE THEIR NAME

Whose name? Everyone's name. Learn everyone's name and use it liberally. If it's a "hard name," then all the more reason to learn it. Usually in introductions, I like to ask something like, "How should I address you?" It typically covers pronouns, preferred names, and the level of formality all in one go. Don't assume the client will use the same naming conventions you are used to.

MAINTAINING CONTROL OF THE CONVERSATION DOESN'T MEAN THERE ISN'T DIALOGUE

As you start interviewing and interacting with clients, you will quickly pick up on how easily things can get off track.

Real-world examples of side topics that have come up in these interviews:

- Seafood buffets.
- How bad the coffee was in our office.
    ◦ It really was though—that may have been a tact more than anything.
- Which department store is better.
- Why the local independently owned pharmacy is closed on Mondays and not Sundays.
- Whether a beloved '90s' children's cartoon character was an aardvark or an anteater.

Ultimately, you as the professional are responsible for gently redirecting the conversation. "We never get anything done because they won't focus" isn't an excuse you can have. You should understand that a fair amount of people will deflect and change topics when they are uncomfortable. If aardvarks and seafood buffets are coming up a lot, it may be an indication that you haven't built up enough rapport to be having difficult conversations.

> *If aardvarks and seafood buffets are coming up a lot, it may be an indication that you haven't built up enough rapport to be having difficult conversations.*

The flip side of that coin is not letting go of the reins of the conversation long enough for the other party to get a word in edgewise—this is my tendency. I'm very much a "look-I-have-so-many-things-to-tell-you-and-show-you-and-oh-look-that's-our-hour" BCBA. My solution was to do caregiver training and meetings more often and have an agenda, so I would have to pause for questions.

◎ EXERCISE 8.1: INTERACTION AGENDA

Write an agenda for a type of client interaction you'd like to improve. It doesn't have to be a formal meeting—you can write one for your pickup/drop-off conversation if applicable. I've filled in one for a caregiver training as an example.

Agenda for a Caregiver Training:

January 22, 2024
Attendees: Jane, Joe, Jack, Jamie, Julia

GETTING STARTED (15 MINUTES)
- Any pressing updates?
- Housekeeping updates (alternative schedule next week)
- Update on action items from the last meeting

TOPICAL DISCUSSION (30 MINUTES)
- Review of progress on mand training programs
- Discussion on motivation
  ◦ Motivation is required for a mand
  ◦ Ways to cultivate motivation at home
  ◦ Satiation = no motivation!
  ◦ Questions/concerns?
- Role-play of mand training with BCBA
  ◦ Include practice with data sheet

REVIEW (15 MINUTES)
- Review graphs and progress updates
- Confirm action items for next caregiver training
- Schedule the next caregiver training

On the next page, practice creating an agenda for a client interation in your experience that you would like to improve.

Agenda for _____

[Date]

[Attendees]

[Opening/Start]   [Time block]

_____

_____

_____

_____

[Topics/Discussion]   [Time block]

_____

_____

_____

_____

[Action Items/Review]   [Time block]

_____

_____

_____

_____

DON'T ARGUE

When a conflict arises with a client, your first thought is probably, "But I'm right." Even if you are, direct contradiction probably isn't going to guide the conversation in the way you would like. On top of that, I've never personally known someone to be converted to the behavior-analytic viewpoint during a heated debate. Here are some things you can do as alternative behaviors to arguing.

- Rephrase their last statement back to them.
  - Caregiver: "This program isn't at all what I thought we would be working on. This is unbelievable."
  - Behavior analyst: "I am hearing your concern that the program isn't what you expected. [Insert explanation as to why the plan changed]."
- If the other person is using a loud, passionate voice, soften yours in both tone and volume. The dramatic difference is an attention grabber, and in my experience, the individual always softens their voice to match mine.
  - This is a fun one to practice with a partner. One person uses a loud, angry voice, and the other responds in a soft, neutral tone. Take turns being in each role. You'll get practice not raising your voice in return and feeling the pull to soften your voice in response to someone speaking softly to you.
- People are naturally inclined to fill silences. It is A-OK to literally pause and not verbally respond for a moment or two when someone is attempting to escalate a situation into an argument. This gives you much needed time to form a thoughtful, professional response while they continue to fill the silence and, in my experience, calm themselves.

WHAT CAN WE LEARN FROM MEDICAL PRACTITIONERS?

Let's look at bedside balance in action with an example from my life. My doctor put me on a medication once, and while it was a medically necessary treatment that benefited me immensely, it was also uncomfortable, and the symptoms were unmanageable. I couldn't live with it, and that felt like a failure on my part. When I went to him, I couldn't articulate what was going on with any kind of medical/biochemical accuracy. I was just able to tell him that I couldn't do this, and it wasn't working. In that moment he did two things that, as clinicians, we can learn from. First, he showed me labs that showed that my being miserable wasn't for nothing—it was working. Second, he gave me a few other options and factually laid out the pros and cons of each, and we decided together how to move forward. He *never* discounted or dismissed what I was saying as not true. He *didn't* talk about how he was the one with the medical degree and this treatment option was what needed to happen And he *didn't* point out that other people went through the same treatment without any problems. On the flip side of that coin, he also *didn't* recommend that I not have any kind of treatment. Being heard, understood, and supported not only helped me feel less miserable, but it also built trust between us and strengthened our patient-provider relationship.

Let's stay in the realm of medicine. I'm sure we all know someone who has had a negative experience or interaction with a doctor. Maybe they felt dismissed, or that their physical pain was minimized. Maybe they weren't given enough education on their treatment, or choice when situations like the above came up. The fact that there are doctors who do the right things like in my story doesn't discount that there are people who have had negative experiences as patients. In healthcare settings, changes are made to policies and procedures to make sure that negative experiences and bad outcomes don't continue to happen (although this can happen at a slower pace than one would like). The same can be said for ABA. We can learn from this model and adapt when we need to.

Now, you may have the instinct to say that ABA is an entirely different world than medicine, and I'd say you are right. But when we are both dealing with prescriptions, referrals, dosage, informed consent, insurance codes and billing, it isn't too much of a stretch to take a page from their playbook on whole person/patient-centered/collaborative care and a model of continued growth and development. When a client brings a concern to you, or tells you something isn't working, *don't* point out that you are the behavior analyst and have a better understanding of behavior; *don't* point out that other people have done the same program and not had concerns; and *don't* implement an all-or-nothing approach.

As a behavior analyst, you are now a clinical practitioner of a life-changing science, with more control over programming and influence on vulnerable populations than you would have had in your fieldwork. With this comes the responsibility to listen and not let your ego prevent you from changing course.

✧ ACTIVITY 8.1: CLIENT CONFLICT DOS AND DON'TS

Instructions: Here are some client conflict dos and don'ts. Circle the dos and cross out the don'ts. *Check your answers on p. 148.*

- Communicate face-to-face
- Assume the person doesn't understand
- Act sooner rather than later
- Be present, clear, and direct
- Get defensive
- Ignore feedback
- Use language that is understandable (no jargon)
- Understand their perspective as well as yours
- Argue feelings
- Focus on the present situation/problem
- Manage your emotions
- Recognize your differences
- Actively listen
- Be honest, genuine, and respectful
- Be aware of body language of all parties
- Avoid the issue
- Interrupt them
- Use put-downs and sarcasm
- Fight about the issue on social media
- Stop communication

QUESTIONS SHOULD GO BEYOND "DO YOU UNDERSTAND?"

Closed-ended questions will give you short answers and low engagement. Now don't get me wrong, I've had some clients who will just jump in whenever they need to, but that isn't everyone's disposition or cultural expectation. As a provider, you need to make the space available.
Potential alternatives to "Do you understand?":

- What are your thoughts on that?
- How does this compare with your experience?
- Before I go any further, I would love to know if you have seen an example of this?

🔍 EXERCISE 8.2: FOSTERING DIALOGUE

Write your own ways to foster dialogue during these types of interactions:

HONESTY THAT ISN'T CRUEL

My son had a therapist early on. She was a great therapist, but we only ever talked when something was wrong: He was misbehaving, or things weren't progressing. Now, most of that was on me—I was always running here or there, and it was notoriously hard to get my full attention in that time of my life, but not impossible. That said, without understanding what was going on from a behavior standpoint, I began to dread hearing how the session went, because if she said more than "great day" post-session, it meant bad news.

Later on, he briefly attended an early preschool program. They had these little take-home notes that I loved. They had what he did and what he ate, and I would look forward to those notes. Then they added a section: "great day," "good day," "try-again day." This was their way of communicating behavior information that needed to be communicated and documented. I am in no way criticizing the program. That said, those try-again days hit like a sucker punch. Although I can't speak for my son, I can imagine if try-again days impacted me significantly, they would have had the same impact on a child who was aware of the system. I stopped looking at the notes when the try-again days started to outweigh the good days.

What both these stories have in common are great service providers who unintentionally diminished my engagement in my son's treatment. My son had many big and small "wins" while working with each of them, but those wins were easily drowned out.

Be honest about the barriers in treatment, but remember to include the positives and even the neutrals to create some balance. Regardless of the type of news you are communicating, include what happened, how it was resolved, and what will be done to prevent (or increase) future incidents. Instead of saying, "He had four tantrums today," you can say, "He had a difficult transition into his first worktable, which we weren't able to fully recover from. We took a lot of breaks to help him relax and calm down. Tomorrow we will have our first worktable a little later in the session to help lessen the stress."

VALIDATE CONCERNS

It can be awkward when clients become emotional, especially early in your career if you don't have much experience. But remember our friend empathy! It's important to be empathetic. At several points, the caregivers of the individuals you work with may be going through grieving processes. Be sure that you are creating a safe space for emotional expression. It's your job not to let it get awkward.

The Don't-Make-It-Awkward Tool Kit:

* Tissues: Stock up!

* Eye contact during conversation (if it is culturally appropriate and comfortable for the individual)

    ◦ BUT avoid eye contact while the individual is blowing their nose.

      - Of course I did that! We both laughed, but I made it weird.

* Open body language

    ◦ Everyone says this, but what does it mean?

      - Don't be busy or multitasking. Your hands and arms can be resting on your desk or at your sides. If you need to fidget, that works too.

      - Try to keep your chest open (shoulders back, not hunched)

      - Direct your chest toward the other person, as if you can draw an imaginary line from their heart to yours.

* Don't be afraid to repeat what they communicated back to them. This helps you understand, gives them the opportunity to clarify, and validates the expression of the emotion.

BEDSIDE BALANCE AND CULTURAL COMPETENCE

As a behavior analyst, you will undoubtedly encounter clients and stakeholders across a variety of cultures. Everything I said above applies; however, treating across cultural backgrounds requires an additional level of nuance.

* **Knowledge of culture:** Behavior analysts should have an awareness of the perspectives, values, traditions, practices, and family systems of the cultures they are working within. In practical terms, this means being aware of the cultural differences between you and your client, listening to them, and trying to work within the cultural system instead of outside of it.

    ◦ As a real-world example, a few years ago, I had a client from a culture that I wasn't familiar with. There wasn't a BCBA at my company, or other local companies, who was more familiar with that culture than I was. Based on the client's needs, it was determined that my skill set was the most appropriate. Since there was no one more culturally competent available, I needed to become culturally competent.

  - One of our goals for the client was that they would appropriately greet individuals. We taught her how to greet staff, teachers, and family members using a variety of "standard" English greetings. I was telling her mother in a progress meeting that we were ready to master out that goal. It was then that her mother asked that we teach a cultural greeting and its response. After a few attempts, it was clear I didn't have a strong grasp on the greeting/response. So, we changed course, and I taught her mother how to teach greetings and intraverbal targets. Since it was a multilingual home, she began using these techniques to teach the other languages used in the home.

- **Education and training:** There are CEUs (see Chapter 11 for more on CEUs) on creating a culturally competent work environment and clinical practice. We also live in a very connected world, so if possible, reach out to other behavior analysts who are more familiar with the culture you are attempting to work within. This works both ways; you can share your cultural background in your team and outside it to help other behavior analysts be culturally competent.

- **Show over tell:**

  - Patient-centered care requires effective communication. In addition to translation services (if required), important messages should be repeated often and in a variety of phrasing.

  - Instead of receiving verbal confirmation (e.g., asking, "Does that make sense?"), have the individual demonstrate the technique or instructions back to you.

- **Hire within the community you serve:**

  - **Representation matters.** You may not be in a position to hire now, but when you are, make sure your team comes from the community you serve.

🎯 EXERCISE 8.3:   CULTURAL REFLECTION

Think critically about your own beliefs, values, and cultural background.

- **Take a moment to define your own culture.**

  - **How do you identify?** This can involve any protected class (e.g., age, race, gender identity, sexual orientation, ethnicity, religion) and/or interests, hobbies, or other aspects of who you are

  - **What assumptions (positive or negative) have people made based on your identity?**

○ **How might your identity lead to implicit bias?** Implicit bias is a nonconscious bias that causes us to gravitate towards familiar things. Having implicit bias doesn't mean you are a "bad person"; it's something everyone has and something to be aware of so you can consciously act against it.

* **Here's my example:**
    ○ I identify as a cisgender female, a mother, a millennial, and a Southerner (i.e., a person from the southern United States).
    ○ People may assume that I eat huge amounts of avocado toast (millennial stereotype) or drive a minivan (something many mothers do, but I don't).
    ○ As a parent, I tend to find common ground easier with other parents, and I need to find commonality more deliberately with nonparents.

THE ELEPHANT IN THE ROOM

ABA is not without its controversies, and part of being balanced at the bedside means being aware and understanding. For the sake of this chapter, what I'm calling controversy is a prolonged and ongoing discussion of an issue, with passionate disagreement. The controversies that were ongoing when I was a new BCBA are likely (hopefully) going to have found resolutions and therefore be different than the ones you encounter throughout your career.

Here's a non-exhaustive list of some of our controversies as a field:

* use of punishment procedures/general aversive conditions
* too much repetition/too little engagement for learners
* too focused on eliminating maladaptive behaviors in lieu of skill building
* focused on forcing neurodiverse individuals to mask
* "dog training for people"

What were your thoughts when you read that list? Did your shoulders tense up? Were you on the verge of sending me a strongly worded email in defense of the field?

Not to overgeneralize, but the controversies I've experienced fall into categories of what we teach and how we teach it.

While your feelings of wanting to "defend" are valid, so are the feelings of the individuals, families, and stakeholders weighing in. Don't fall into the temptation to say, "They don't understand" or "I'm the professional." They understand the impact of the application of the science on them, and how it makes them feel.

🎯 EXERCISE 8.4: BEDSIDE BALANCE REFLECTION

Go through the following questions with your last client interaction in mind.

- Did my last interaction with said client/caregiver/stakeholder involve exclusively generic terms (great/good/bad) when describing the client and/or their progress?

- Did my last interaction involve specific labeling of barriers, maladaptive behavior, or corrective feedback?

  ○ If so, did this communication of barriers, maladaptive behavior, or corrective feedback come before a *neutral* or *positive* statement?

  ○ Was I multitasking when I communicated this information?

  ○ Was the other party expected to be multitasking (e.g., the client was already transferred to their care, or I was speaking while they were filling out forms)?

- Did I give the individual time to respond to my statements and ask questions?

- Was I the person to terminate the interaction (e.g., "Well that's all," "Have a great day," looking at the door or shifting away from the individual I was speaking to)?

- Did I use terms that I am not confident the other party understands (ABA or formal language)?

  ○ Have I accounted for, or even asked about, communication preferences?

  ○ Have I accounted for translation/interpretation services, should they be required?

SURVIVAL BASICS

This is a dense chapter with a lot to unpack. I hope you continue to refer back to this through your first year and beyond. Bedside balance isn't something that snaps into place. It takes time and continuous energy to evolve. As a BCBA (and just as a human), I have put my foot in my mouth too many times to count. Being balanced in your interactions isn't about never flubbing or being awkward—it's about empowering your clients. After all, as Maya Angelou said, "People will forget what you said, people will forget what you did, but people will never forget how you made them feel" (Angelou, 2014, p. 41).

CHAPTER 9

Collaboration With Service Professionals

When I became a BCBA, I didn't take any coursework on *collaboration*. I went out into the behavior-analytic universe having limited experience working with other service professionals. Collaboration, however, has been absolutely vital in my work as a BCBA. I've collaborated with a wide variety of other professions, and you are likely to do so as well. So, let's meet some of your potential team members.

MEET THE TEAM

Speech-language pathologist (SLP) or "speech therapist": SLPs work with a wide range of clients in varied settings (hospitals, schools, skilled nursing facilities, clinics—sound familiar?). No matter what healthcare setting you work in, you are likely to find an SLP. They can work on speech production, language and communication, oral motor, feeding, and the list goes on. There is extensive overlap between our areas of expertise.

Occupational therapist (OT): OTs also work with a wide variety of individuals in multiple settings (hospitals, schools, skilled nursing facilities, clinics). Occupational therapy focuses on the whole person and their ability to complete tasks in their daily lives. Some examples of what an occupational therapist could address are motor skills and sensory difficulties.

Physical therapist (PT): PTs, too, work with a wide range of individuals and settings (hospitals, schools, skilled nursing facilities, clinics). Physical therapists work with clients to improve their mobility and function, generally through movement and exercise.

Primary care provider (PCP): A PCP is a physician, nurse practitioner, or nursing specialist who provides and coordinates healthcare services. This person is the medical "home" for the individual. For example, a child's PCP would be their pediatrician. This doctor would provide wellness checks, vaccines, and treatment when the child is sick. If referrals to specialists or therapy (ABA) are needed, they would most likely come from the PCP.

Prescribing physician: A prescribing physician is a physician who prescribes and monitors medication. In ABA you'll see this in the context of psychotropic medications.

Note that this is not an exhaustive list. You may get the opportunity to collaborate with many other professionals, or not interact with everyone I have listed above. It is all dependent upon your work contexts. I have not included non-service professionals in the list (caregivers, teachers, childcare professionals); however, the principles will still apply.

Before diving into the "how," let's start by establishing what collaboration is.

DEFINING COLLABORATION

🎯 EXERCISE 9.1:   DEFINITIONS AND REFLECTION

Thinking about your personal and professional experiences, provide your own definition of collaboration:

Kelly and Tincani (2013) provide an operational definition of collaboration:

66

"Voluntary... interactions comprising of two or more professionals engaging in communication modalities for the purposes of shared decision-making and problem solving ... that would not have been achieved in isolation" [emphasis added] (p. 129).

99

Reflect on this definition
Why is it best for collaboration to be *voluntary*?

How does collaboration promote *shared decision-making*?

In your experience, what is an example of a solution that would not have been achieved in *isolation*?

My reflection

Why is it best for collaboration to be *voluntary*? Once, I had the "mandatory opportunity" to collaborate with a few other BCBAs at the company I was in. It was an amazing experience, but the fact that so many of us were pulled from our other work to collaborate caused tensions to run high during the project.

How does collaboration promote *shared decision-making*? If only one person is making the decision, then that's more like delegation than collaboration. No one likes it when their ideas aren't incorporated or appreciated.

In your experience, what is an example of a solution that would not have been achieved in *isolation*? I had a client who was a very bouncy little girl. I had a hard time having her remain seated long enough to train some receptive targets. I was starting to burn through my bag of tricks. We had an in-house OT who served the client as well. She and I came together, and she was able to do some assessments and find alternative seating that solved the problem without me having to do any kind of traditional "duration in seat" protocols.

EVIDENCE-BASED PRACTICE

I've encountered some early BCBAs who thought that "evidence-based" was synonymous with "behavior-analytic." While we only use evidence-based practices in ABA, it doesn't mean that other professions *don't* use evidence-based practices and procedures. It's one of those all-squares-are-rectangles-but-not-all-rectangles-are-squares situations.

HANDS-ON COLLABORATION TO ACHIEVE GOALS

You may never "see" your clients' other service providers. I've had a few clients whose other providers declined to have meetings, or everyone's busy schedules just didn't allow for the type of collaboration we both would have liked. Even in situations like those, I could "see" those individuals in my clients' plans of care. *Compliance note: Remember that clients need to sign release forms before you exchange clinical documentation with another service provider.*

◎ EXERCISE 9.2: IDENTIFYING AND RESPECTING OTHERS' GOALS

Which goal was written by a behavior analyst? Circle the goal and describe the rationale.

1. CLIENT will consistently produce the oral stop consonants /t/ /d/ /k/ /g/ as measured by 80% correct responding by the end of the treatment period.

2. CLIENT will independently echo the consonant sounds /p/ /b/ /g/ /k/ as measured by 100% correct responding across three consecutive sessions with a 7-day retention check.

Rationale:

_____

_____

The word "echo" was likely the clue that the second goal was taken from an ABA clinical plan of care. Those familiar with speech-language pathology would also have recognized "oral stop consonants" in the first goal.

The goal (#2) written by a behavior analyst:

- has higher mastery criteria (McDougale et al., 2020),
- has measurable and specific criteria,
- passes the "dead man's test," and
- has a retention probe.

The goal (#1) written by an SLP:

- has lower mastery criteria, although it should be noted that we often see those lower criteria in ABA goals (McDougale et al., 2020),
- has measurable and specific criteria
- passes the "dead man's test," and
- has a more dynamic clustering of speech sounds, per speech-language pathology literature (DeVeney et al., 2020).

Which goal was written by a behavior analyst? Circle the goal and describe the rationale.

1. CLIENT will cut on a curved line within ¼ inch deviation in three out of four trials, independently.

2. CLIENT will cut across paper with scissors 100% of opportunities across three consecutive sessions.

Rationale:

Now I think it is easy to point out that neither one of these goals is particularly detailed, but both were pulled from actual treatment plans. I prefer the first goal, which was written by an OT. I find the inclusion of the ¼ inch deviation to be helpful in labeling what cutting means at this point in time.

The second goal was written by a behavior analyst. While the mastery criteria are higher, the definition of cutting and what constitutes "across paper" leaves too much room for interpretation.

Which goal was written by a behavior analyst? Circle the goal and describe the rationale.

1. CLIENT will be able to identify all coins associated with U.S. currency 100% of opportunities for five consecutive sessions.

2. CLIENT will, by the end of the [x period], match coins (penny, nickel, dime, quarter) with a variety of materials (book, cards, real coins) with 70% accuracy and 100% independence as measured by collected data.

Rationale:

This was a little bit of a trick question. The first goal was written by a behavior analyst, and the second goal came from an IEP (see Chapter 10 for more on IEPs). While the mastery criteria are higher in the goal written by the behavior analyst, the inclusion of the data method and the generalization across modalities are things you should think about as a behavior analyst. With goals, it is better to be more specific than leave room for interpretation.

TIPS TO GO FORTH AND COLLABORATE

1. Get to know the profession of others you work with in your setting and area. Introduce yourself and ask to learn more about what they do.

2. Discuss common goals you have for your client and how you can collaborate.

3. Create a collaboration goal with someone outside of your field.

4. If appropriate, ask for a demonstration of a strategy or intervention, so you can see for yourself what is being done, and offer to show how you would implement interventions for the same goal. Then discuss the commonalities and/or differences in strategies.

5. Set regular collaboration meetings and have an agenda where concerns, successes, and progress are discussed.

6. Offer help with your skills that are applicable across all fields, such as data collection strategies, graphing, operational definitions, measurement of behavior, skill acquisition, and progress monitoring.

7. Stay open to learning from others without compromising your ethical obligations as a professional.

SURVIVAL BASICS

I heard a joke while attending the Florida Association for Behavior Analysis (FABA) annual conference that went something like "A BCBA, an occupational therapist, and a speech therapist walk into a conference. They all introduce themselves. The occupational therapist says, "Good Morning! I teach people to manage their sensory needs." The speech therapist says, "Hello! I teach people to communicate and eat." The BCBA is last and says, "Nice to meet you; I'm better than all of you." Like all jokes, there's a piece of hyperbolized truth in it. Let's face it, behavior analysis can seem elitist. We've invented enough new terms to fill a few dictionaries. Keep this idea in mind as you go forward in your collaboration. That, along with learning and respecting the foundational knowledge of other professions, will go a long way in setting you up for productive collaborations.

CHAPTER 10

IEP Meeting Expectations

The *Individualized Education Program* (or sometimes, Plan) (IEP) outlines goals for a student throughout the academic year and specifies any support they'll need to reach them. This could include extending the child's school year through summer periods. The IEP is developed by a team of professionals but is designed to include the caregivers' input.

You will encounter an IEP if you have school-age clients who attend a public school and meet the requirements for one. You may have clients you never attend an IEP meeting for, and others for whom you attend every year—the deciding factor on that is the caregiver. A child's IEP must be reviewed at least annually.

The overarching goal of the IEP is to provide the child access to the general education curriculum (when appropriate, it may be recommended that the child go to an alternative curriculum) and to allow the student to be successful in the *least restrictive environment*. I like to think of the least restrictive environment as least-to-most prompting. As behavior analysts, we can manipulate the environment as we see fit, while schools are bound by the least restrictive environment. Understanding the goals of the program and the overarching philosophy behind it will help you understand where you might disagree. If you do disagree on how your client's school is handling maladaptive behavior, I cannot stress enough how important it is to have a gentle hand and understand that it is not your environment to manipulate as you please.

A behavior analyst's role in the development of an IEP is dependent on their relationship to the school. Behavior analysts working in the school as consultants will likely have direct or indirect input into the program. A behavior analyst who is working with a school-age client privately may be asked to provide input, but that isn't a normal occurrence in my experience.

Most caregivers I've encountered have felt intimidated and underprepared for the IEP process. Unfortunately, the IEP process can be rather complex and initially time intensive.

You may have caregivers coming to you for support and help as they navigate this process. Even if you feel confident answering the question, it is best to redirect them to resources from the Department of Education for your state.

TRIVIA

What is the difference between an IEP and an Individualized Family Service Plan (IFSP)?

- An *IEP* is developed for eligible children with disabilities ages 3 through 21 and includes special education and related services; it's designed to meet the child's unique needs and prepare the child for further education, employment, and independent living.

- An *IFSP* is a written plan for providing early intervention services to an infant or toddler with a disability and their family.

(U.S. Department of Education, n.d.-a)

BEFORE AN IEP MEETING

When a student has special educational needs, they are referred for an evaluation for special education services. Keep in mind that special education is a service, not a place (aka specific classroom). So, the first step in the process is not necessarily putting together an IEP. If a student is identified as potentially benefiting from special education services, a referral is made, and a consent form is provided to caregivers. The evaluation for special needs services *requires* caregiver consent and is usually done at the school district level. This means that the evaluation *may* not be done at the child's home school.

The professionals conducting the evaluation are likely to come from a variety of disciplines, which may include a school psychologist, an SLP, an OT, a PT, a behavior analyst, and more, depending on the child's needs. Together, they will determine if the child needs special education services.

Children who receive special education services are documented as having an *exceptionality*. It should be noted that these are different than medical diagnoses. Just because your client has a medical diagnosis does not necessarily mean they will have an exceptionality. For example, your client may have a diagnosis of autism but require no support in the classroom; they therefore would not meet the criteria for an exceptionality. This hasn't happened often in my experience, but it has happened. If the caregiver disagrees with the outcome of the evaluation, they can request an *independent educational evaluation* (IEE) conducted by someone outside the school system.

Once eligibility is established, an IEP meeting will be set within 30 days. Caregivers are notified in advance and can bring any advocate they would like, including you. Keep in mind and remind caregivers if they invite you (in writing) that they must provide the school with advance notice (in writing) of whom they intend to bring. The rule of thumb I've heard is 2 weeks, but this is likely to vary by school district.

DURING AN IEP MEETING

The IEP meeting is partially developed before the meeting and then finalized *during the meeting*. The first step in IEP development is usually gathering available assessment information about the child. The caregivers may provide documentation you have given them, like treatment plans, graphs, or programs, to the school at this point. If caregivers specifically come to me and ask for documentation that would be helpful to give the school, I will usually draft up basic interaction guides, gather assessment scores, and provide information about the maladaptive behaviors. I intentionally *do not* include goals, as goals used for insurance purposes need to be distinct from goals on an IEP. They can coordinate, but they cannot be identical. I've had school districts copy and paste my goals more than once, and then I had to rewrite a treatment plan on the fly. It was not fun.

The IEP may also contain some form of benchmarking, which may or may not overlap with some of the assessments we use in clinical practice. I have worked with some school districts that use VB-MAPP and some that use ABLLS-R. An initial IEP will have measurable annual goals, the child's current academic performance, how and how often services will be provided, and if any education aids will be utilized (things like assistive technology). Now, there isn't a menu caregivers can choose from, so it can be hard to know what supports are available. I caution against providing caregivers with a makeshift menu yourself. The IEP process can become complex and contentious quickly, and you do not want to provide inaccurate information to a family that leads to high conflict between them and the school. You can prompt them to ask for what is available and communicate openly and often with the school. That said, if the communication isn't going well, you can support them by teaching them to be their own advocate or providing them with connections to local advocates should they need them. You can also direct them to information from the Department of Education and from your local school board.

What Should You Do at an IEP Meeting?

Sit there and be quiet. You are there as a guest of the caregiver. When your opinion is asked you can respond, but don't be surprised if no one asks for it. I like to bring a legal pad so that if I have a question that I believe the caregiver should ask, I can discreetly show them, and they can ask. This is a place to leave your ego at the door—it isn't your show or your decision.

> *This is a place to leave your ego at the door—it isn't your show or your decision.*

Once, I attended an IEP meeting in a district I wasn't familiar with. The caregivers were new to IEPs and very nervous. Prior to the IEP meeting, I like to meet and review expectations and walk in together. When we arrived, the school district was ... cold, to put it nicely. They were amazing and the IEP was great; they just didn't want me there. You may think, "Oh Mariah, you're being silly," but hear me out: Everyone had an adult chair but me, and everyone was seated around a table, and they had me in a literal corner. It didn't help that every time they asked the caregivers to sign off on something, the caregivers looked at me for approval. I kept on smiling and didn't make it about me. I understand that the likely reason for the cold shoulder is they have been told off by a few too many behavior analysts, and "BCBA" became an S^D (discriminative stimulus). The saving grace in this situation was when the OT who consulted for the school system came in to review her portion of the IEP. I recognized her from other cases, and we greeted each other warmly. She asked for my input, and we openly *collaborated* (see, it is important!) for her portion of the meeting. It defrosted the rest of the room.

✎ ACTIVITY 10.1: IEP DOS AND DON'TS

Instructions: Circle the dos and cross out the don'ts. *Check your answers on p. 149.*

Bring the client's relevant records with you.

Bring the most recent graphs and behavior intervention plan (BIP).

Speak in jargon.

Impress all the teachers by using as many behavior-analytic words as possible.

Assume the school, private therapy team, and caregivers are on the same team.

Be defensive if nobody wants to see your BIP.

Be flexible and respectful of the team's time.

Read reports provided to you.

ACRONYMS IN AN IEP MEETING

Legend has it that the only time a behavior analyst can get "out-acronym-ed" is at an IEP meeting. I've compiled acronyms you're likely to hear at an IEP meeting here, but be sure to head over to the glossary for a more comprehensive acronym listing.

Approved private school (APS): Schools approved to provide a free and appropriate education for students with severe disabilities.

Community-based instruction (CBI): Data-driven, guided outing that occurs in a natural setting where the student can work toward an IEP goal. CBI most often happens in placements where the student is in a life skills program.

Early intervention (EI): A process of assessment and therapy provided to children, especially those younger than age 3.

Emotional disturbance (ED): An IEP exceptionality. Emotional disturbance means the child may have inappropriate types of behaviors or feelings under normal circumstances, a general and pervasive mood of unhappiness, and a tendency to develop fears around school and to a marked degree that adversely affects their educational performance. Some states refer to this exceptionality as emotional behavior disturbance (EBD).

Extended school year (ESY): An extension of the school district's or charter school's traditional school year to provide special education and related services to a student with a disability, per the student's IEP, and at no cost to the student's caregivers.

Free appropriate public education (FAPE): The right to FAPE is a powerful legal right for children with disabilities. FAPE requires schools to provide special education to meet the unique needs of a child.

Functional behavior assessment (FBA): A process rooted in the science of ABA that focuses on gathering relevant data and information to determine the function of behavior to design a function-based intervention that will maximize the effectiveness and efficiency of behavior support.

Individualized Education Program (IEP): A document developed for special needs children by their caregivers and educators. The plan is provided at no cost to caregivers and is required in all public and private schools receiving public funds for the education of children with disabilities.

Least restrictive environment (LRE): A guiding principle in the Individuals with Disabilities Education Act (IDEA). Therefore, LRE plays a critical role in determining where the student will spend their time in school and how special education services will be provided.

Multi-tiered system of supports (MTSS): A framework many schools use to provide specific support to struggling students. The goal of MTSS is to intervene early to assist students in achieving grade-level standards, by focusing on the whole child.

SURVIVAL BASICS

Although you may not directly attend an IEP meeting, you will likely serve some clients who receive special education services at some point. Here are a few things to keep in mind.

- Special education is a service, not a place.

- A medical diagnosis is not the same as an exceptionality.

- Goals in private clinical practice should not be identical to goals in an IEP, but they may be complementary.

- Redirect caregivers to appropriate official resources for their IEP questions and concerns.

✎ ACTIVITY 10.2: IEP ACRONYM CROSSWORD

Instructions: Try your hand at the crossword below. Note that a hyphen counts as a space. *Check your answers on p. 150.*

CLUES

ACROSS			DOWN	
2. ESY	4. IEP	9. LRE	1. FAPE	6. ED
3. APS	8. CBI	10. FBA	5. MTSS	7. EI

CHAPTER 11

Cycling Through CEUs

I worked with a fellow BCBA during my first year in clinical practice—we earned our certification at the same time. We were, and remain, close friends. I have her permission to share stories about her relationship with CEUs (also called *continuing education units,* or CEs) early in her career. For her privacy, we will call her Patricia.

I had been worrying about recertification from the moment I was certified—you could call me a nervous type. Patricia is the natural opposite. One day I was wondering aloud, to our director of staff development, how I was going to earn all the required ethics CEU courses. At that point, we had been BCBAs for just shy of a year. Patricia scrunched her face, looked from me to our director, and asked, "What's a CEU?" That was the inspiration for this chapter.

As a certified behavior analyst, you now have a certification to keep up. One of the ways you'll do that is by taking continuing education coursework. The amount you will need to maintain your credential is likely to change over time. It's important to stay up to date on the BACB requirements. Look up and fill in the requirements for your recertification cycle below. Note that the requirements usually involve a certain amount of ethics and supervision coursework hours.

🎯 EXERCISE 11.1:   RECERTIFICATION REQUIREMENTS

Look up the requirements for your recertification cycle and fill in the table below. I've filled in the first table as an example.

Recertification Date	Requirement: ETHICS	Requirement: SUPERVISION	Requirement: GENERAL
2-28-23	4 Units	3 Units	32 Units

Your recertification information:

Recertification Date	Requirement:	Requirement:	Requirement:

EARNING CEUS

It's important to get your CEUs from a reputable and approved provider. How do you know which organizations are reputable and approved? The Authorized Continuing Education (ACE) program helps you identify which providers are authorized by the BACB. If your CEU comes from an ACE provider, it is an approved CEU. Lists of authorized organizations can be found on the BACB website.

There are a variety of ways to access CEUs, and we will talk about each in depth.

• Conferences

• Virtual CEUs

• Company-provided workshops

You can also gain CEUs by teaching or completing academic coursework. You aren't likely to encounter those CEU types in your first year, though, so we'll focus on the three listed above.

Conferences

Different types and sizes of organizations can put on conferences, including local behavioral companies, county/state chapters of ABA organizations, and national and international organizations. They can be on the pricier side and might not be financially accessible to you early on in your career. Check to see if your employer will provide a stipend or otherwise assist you in attending conferences. Most organizations will have some form of CEU compensation/stipend.

Conferences generally have four different types of session formats:

• **Keynote (or plenary) presentations**

  ○ These presentations are often given by well-known speakers. Most participants will attend the keynote—I've rarely seen anything else scheduled at the same time. The keynote will usually offer CEUs; check your conference program.

• **Panel sessions**

  ○ Panel sessions have multiple presenters who discuss the same or related topics. Panel sessions usually offer CEUs; check your conference program.

• **Poster sessions**

  ○ In a poster session, a researcher explains a poster they've produced displaying a summary of their research, using usually a mixture of text with images, graphs, tables, etc. Typically, poster sessions have multiple presenters/posters set up within a designated area. I've been to some poster sessions that were worth CEUs and some that weren't; check your conference program.

- **Conference paper presentations**
  - ○ Researchers present a paper and invite and respond to feedback from the audience. These are usually grouped into topics or parallel streams. When I have encountered these, they have been for CEUs; check your conference program.

Making the most of your conference

1. **Make a plan.** Conferences are where my type A comes to play. Know what your requirements are and what you would like to get out of the conference from a continuing education standpoint. Most conferences publish programs in advance so you can plan out your day(s). I come with a list of the CEUs I need, plan those, and then choose what else I want to see based on personal preference.

2. **You don't need to attend every talk, poster session, and panel.** Plan out your breaks. At the time I was a new BCBA, a total of 32 hours of continuing education was required for a 2-year cycle. My colleague Patricia promptly forgot about our earlier CEU conversation, and in our second year as BCBAs, we went to the FABA conference. She needed all her CEUs—and got them all over the 3-day conference—because she was only a few weeks out from her recertification. She was there 7:00 a.m.–9:00 p.m. and barely stopped to eat. In retrospect, she could have done some online coursework after the conference so that she didn't *need* to subject herself to that conference marathon-style. In the end it was a great story and an exhausting weekend, but not something you want to repeat as you earn CEUs.

3. **Network.** Even though you can't earn CEUs just for meeting people, going to conference socials is a part of the fun. If you are hoping to connect with specific individuals or interest groups, reach out to coordinate in advance. Social media is a great way to connect prior to a conference.

Virtual CEUs

More and more of our continuing education is taking place virtually. This can present a convenient and accessible option; it's one that I utilize extensively. There are both live and prerecorded CEU options out there. Pricing can vary depending on the provider and length of training.

Making the most of your virtual continuing education

1. **Set a schedule.** Yes, you're incredibly busy. It's a wonder any of us has the time to pursue continuing education, but it is necessary. Instead of leaving your required hours to the last minute, schedule them into your year—ideally multiple times a year.

2. **Give yourself a dedicated space.** And I do not mean at the kitchen table (if you can help it). Instead, you need a quiet place where you can close the door so that no one disturbs you. Or, at the very least, you need a spot where, when your family sees you working, they know it's "don't bug you" time. Several of you may be working on continuing education credits in clinic offices. The closed-door trick comes in handy there too.

🎯 EXERCISE 11.2:   S△S

I love a good S△ (S-delta) sign. Take a second to design one of your own to keep others at bay while class is in session. I've included an example to inspire you.

Please
DO NOT DISTURB
or I won't get any work done

3. **Turn off the phone ...** and email, and messaging apps, and all of the infinite ways you can be contacted.

4. **Take courses that interest you.** This will provide you with the motivation to focus and get the most out of your experience.

5. **Consider partnering with a study buddy.** In full honesty, this tip doesn't work as well for me as it has for others I work with. I tend to be very attention-motivated and tempted to chat the entire time. That said, I have hosted CEU movie nights in the past. For these "movie nights," we would play a virtual CEU on the projector in the office and eat snacks. Those who wanted credit would have to complete the ASRs on their own laptops. We had much more fun than we would have if we had done it individually, and it was a great team-building exercise.

6. **Take notes!** Take it from me that you will not remember as much as you would like to.

> *Instead of leaving your required hours to the last minute, schedule them into your year—ideally multiple times a year.*

Company-Provided Workshops

Company-provided workshops look different at each organization. I have gone to some that are almost like self-contained conferences, while others are much more intimate. These are almost always free to employees and will be worth CEUs if your organization is an ACE provider. These tend to have the added benefit of facilitating team building.

Which Courses Should I Take?

There are an infinite number of choices in CEUs. Outside of meeting the requirements set by the BACB, I like to use six categories when picking my courses.

🎯 EXERCISE 11.3:   CEU CATEGORIES

My categories are:

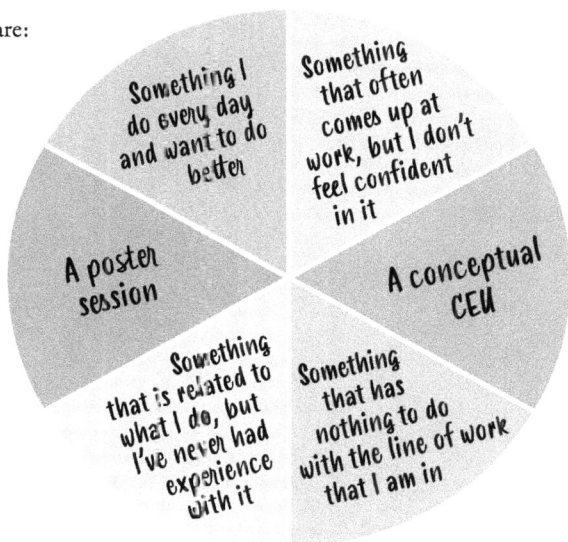

Use the template below to create your own categories and color them in when you've completed them.

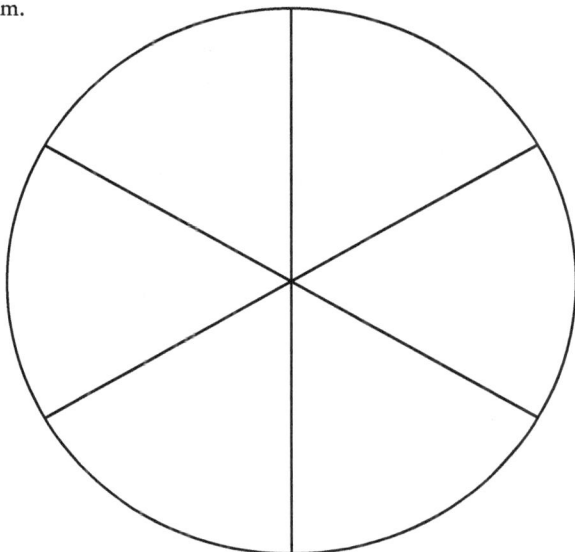

You've Taken the Course—Now What?

After you take a continuing education course and meet any other requirements (e.g., complete a satisfaction survey or quiz), your ACE provider will provide you with a learning certificate (or a CE certificate). Below is an example. The majority, if not all, of the information on the learning certificate will be filled out by the provider. The turnaround time can vary, with some being instant and others taking around 30 days.

Figure 11.1: *CE Certificate Example*

You will need to keep these records and enter them on your BACB account. At the writing of this chapter, there aren't any requirements regarding how quickly you need to update your BACB account. That said, I recommend booking time in your calendar to do this the same week you receive your learning certificate. For storage, I recommend a file on your computer or a fireproof safe in your home.

It's been almost a decade since Patricia and I went to our first conference together. We try to go together at least every other year, and I'd like to be able to say we are old pros now, but that wouldn't exactly be true. I no longer worry over my CEUs, and Patricia no longer tries to get 2 years' worth in 3 days, but I am writing this chapter in an office with a stack of unentered CE certificates next to me. Still—progress, right?

SURVIVAL BASICS

When it comes to surviving CEUs, there are only a few things you need to keep in mind.

- Don't try to pull a Patricia without a big water bottle and protein bars (kidding).
- Know what your requirements are (check with the BACB):
  - Make a plan for how you will complete these requirements. Match the requirements with things you actually need/want to learn.
  - Set yourself up for success by scheduling breaks and being in an environment where you can focus.
- Keep records to prove you actually completed these requirements.

TOOL 11.1: CEU NOTE PAGES

Patricia had an art background and would make beautiful note pages. I wouldn't miss an opportunity to use some of her notepaper in conferences. I love looking back on the notes and being able to reference them afterward. I've included some note pages that follow for you to use on your CEU journey.

CEU Notes Sheet

Course name   Date

KEY IDEAS

CEU Notes Sheet

Course name   Date

KEY IDEAS

CEU Notes Sheet

Course name   Date

KEY IDEAS

CEU Notes Sheet

Course name   Date

KEY IDEAS

CHAPTER 12

What to Do When You Don't Know What to Do

Ever heard of Adriaan de Groot? Before you check Cooper et al. (2020), he wasn't a behavior analyst. He was a psychologist and chess master. In one of his experiments in the 1940s, he had chess masters and amateurs try to memorize how pieces were laid out on a chessboard. The chess masters were able to do this a lot better than the amateurs (de Groot, 1978).

Later, his work was replicated and expanded on by Herbert Simon and William Chase. They added a condition where the pieces on the board were in completely random positions that wouldn't have come up in game play. In this condition the masters didn't fare any better than the amateurs (Simon & Chase, 1973).

These studies were specific in their objectives and not intended for broad application for what to do as a behavior analyst. I bring them up only to illustrate that with familiarity comes an advantage, but a limited one. No matter how much you know, there will always be more that you don't know.

I DON'T KNOW WHAT TO DO

In starting this new venture, familiarity probably isn't on your side yet—yes, even after *all* those field experience hours. It's very tempting to lean into overconfidence and lose all footing when something goes wrong. I know firsthand. I had a client in my first years who was the same age and had the same combination of diagnoses that I considered to be my "bread and butter." I was overly confident, and it caused some stumbling blocks along the way that could have been avoided had I been looking, listening, and reacting the way I should have been.

Just about everything is easier when you have some options to choose from, like how multiple choice questions can seem easier than short answer ones (aka cued recall vs. free recall). In that spirit, I'm giving you some yes/no questions as a jumping-off point.

☼ TOOL 12.1: THE I DON'T KNOW WHAT TO DO BREAKDOWN

Instructions: To help figure out what to do next, ask yourself these questions. For any questions you answer "yes" to, head to the corresponding section(s) below.

Do you know what the problem is?	Yes/No
Do you have enough information?	Yes/No
Are you panicking?	Yes/No
Is the problem related to a client?	Yes/No
Do you know how to program for the goal/behavior?	Yes/No
Do you know where to access journals?	Yes/No
Can you narrow down what you should do first?	Yes/No

I Don't Know What the Problem Is

Admitting you don't know what the problem is, is a good first step. Thinking backwards can be a good problem-solving technique and open up options you didn't think of during the first go-around. What are the consequences of the problem? When did the problem start?

Whatever the symptoms (or consequences if you are working backwards) are, think about what could be causing it. Just take some guesses to get started in your problem-solving (*just* your problem-solving, not your actual work with clients). If you have a guess, you can prove or disprove it later.

I Don't Have Enough Information

Go get some more information. Easier said than done, right? It's more helpful if you know what questions to ask. If you have one question you are stuck on, ask it in different ways and see how the question evolves.

☼ TOOL 12.2: TURNING QUESTIONS INTO MORE QUESTIONS

Instructions: If you are stuck without an answer, it could be because you aren't asking the right (or right number of) question(s). Write the question you are stuck on as the starting question and then brainstorm additional, related questions. I went through one as an example to get you started.

Example:

Starting question:
Why is the behavior targeted for reduction so unpredictable?
↓
Why is the replacement behavior inconsistent?
↓
Where is the reinforcement for the replacement behavior?
↓
What are the antecedents when the replacement behavior does/doesn't occur?

Your turn! Take some time to turn one question into three.

Starting question:

_____

↓

_____

↓

_____

↓

_____

Now write what you think the answers to those questions are. Take a guess. Sometimes it's easier to take a hypothesis and prove it wrong than to wait for the tally sheet to miraculously tell you the answer. Take what you wrote above and try to prove yourself wrong. This is a problem-solving exercise. Caution: If this is for a client, this one exercise is *not* enough to make clinical decisions.

_____

_____

_____

_____

Repeat this question and answer process until you have narrowed it down, and then go back to the breakdown above.

I Am Panicking

The first thing you need to do is slow things down. When I realize I have no idea what to do, that is usually when the panic is setting in. Notice that I used the present tense. This doesn't really stop happening—at least it hasn't for me yet.

- Panic causes problems and usually sets in before you realize it. Is your heart beating quickly? Can you feel a pounding pulse somewhere that isn't your chest? Then it's time to address that *before* making any decisions. You usually have more time than you think.

  - You can slow things down with a big ol' deep breath.
  - Try to lower your heart rate if you feel it spiking. Breathe in through the nose and out through the mouth.
  - I like to put on hand lotion. I've found it to be grounding to both *feel* something and *smell* it, but that is dependent on the situation. I can't always whip out hand lotion in the middle of dealing with a severe behavior event.

- I meant it when I said you have more time than you think.

  - When do you need a resolution?
  - What are the consequences if the issue is not resolved by that deadline?

Feeling better? Drink some water, have a snack, and go back to the breakdown.

The Problem Is Related to a Client

Problems that are related to clients are typically a lot more complicated than other problems. In these cases, you always want to pull in another behavior analyst if you can.

I Don't Know How to Program for a Goal/Behavior

The good news is that even if you've never seen a behavior before, someone else probably has. Do you have someone in your organization who you can reach out to? With how spread out we are as a field, you may not have the opportunity to work with many BCBAs with diverse experience. While I hope that isn't the case, we do have something that connects the work we all do: journals! An academic journal is a *peer-reviewed periodical* in which researchers publish their entries, news, or reports in the form of articles. Journals deal with scholarly publications in various fields including both quantitative and qualitative sciences. Our field's relationship to journals goes all the way back to our experimental psychology days. These articles disseminate tools, techniques, and opinions, and ultimately shape our field.

There are different types of articles that can be found in journals, and they can vary across journals. At the writing of this chapter, *JABA* is one of the leading journals for ABA, and as such I'm using the types of manuscripts that can be submitted for publication in that journal (JABA, n.d.).

- **Research articles:** These are what you typically think of when you think of journal articles. You probably read 100 of these for school.

- **Replications:** These articles describe original research experiments and the results of the author's repetition and expansion of those experiments.

- **Discussion articles:** These articles evaluate/interpret certain research issues or areas of interest.

- **Concise reviews:** These articles review literature on a specific topic. The focus is usually narrow as it provides direction for future research.

- **Technical reports:** These articles focus on procedures, analysis, or other instrumentation.

- **Book reviews:** These are book reports that you, as the reader, don't have to write.

As the research is always evolving, we should be looking at it quarterly when it comes out. I understand that time is a valuable commodity, and it will feel like you don't have enough of it to read articles. If you are dealing with a clinical issue, narrow down your time investment and check journals for research articles, replications, and technical reports first.

Social media, ABA podcasts, CEUs, and journal clubs can cut down on the time/effort investment of staying up to date with the research. At the writing of this chapter, there are tons of social media pages/groups where behavior analysts can gather and connect. These are a great way to find ongoing supervision and find special interest groups. I do want to caution against bringing specific clients/cases/uncomfortable professional situations on to social media, for ethical and privacy reasons.

I Don't Know Where to Access Journals

Journals are how academics communicate with each other and provide a lasting legacy for the growth and expansion of the field. They give us a shared language and dialogue. Publishing in journals outside of behavior analysis helps disseminate ideas with other disciplines. Skinner wrote approximately 180 articles in various journals. He was a prolific writer. His writings still shape how many people view our field, and he is the reason for all the pigeon jokes.

At the writing of this chapter, journal access is included in the BCBA certification. You can find journals by logging into your BACB account. If you are affiliated with a university, you can also access them through the university library. Agencies and companies sometimes subscribe to journals; check with your administrator. Journals and article access are also available for purchase, but they can be a bit pricey.

Let's break down the pieces of a journal article. Original research and replications typically have these parts.

Abstract

The abstract is essentially a spoiler recap of the article that you read before the article. Read this part to determine if the article is relevant to the question you need to answer.

Introduction

The introduction looks at the area of interest being addressed in the study and why it is important. This will also help you determine how relevant the question is for you.

Method

This section is essentially the recipe of the experiment. It provides information on the participants, setting, variables, methods for data collection, interobserver agreement calculations, experimental design, and methods. This is the how-to of the article. If you want to try and repeat the techniques in the article, you will need to pay special attention to the methodology.

Results

This has the graphs and any tabular data. This will tell you how effective the research methodologies were.

Discussion

The author gives you key takeaways from the article and explains any tabular data. This portion will also include areas for future research and limitations of the study. Pay special attention to this section if you plan on replicating the article.

The Problem Is Not Related to a Client

The good news is that you can be more flexible in how you approach this situation. Brainstorm what the problem is and what potential solutions you have.

- Identify and define the problem.
- Come up with possible solutions.
- Evaluate the options.
- Choose the best solution.
- Implement the solution.
- Evaluate the outcome.

I Need to Narrow Down What I Should Do

You can't do all the things all the time. What do you need to accomplish? Usually, we have a lot of things we are trying to accomplish at once, and it muddies the waters. Pick one thing to accomplish and problem-solve it. Every early behavior analyst I've ever met has immediately tried to remediate all the symptoms and improve every aspect of quality of life at the same time. It's a noble effort, but it's no wonder they are exhausted a few months in. Narrow your focus and strategies: Is there one thing you can do that will solve about 60% of the problem? This is a great time to reach out and ask for help from another BCBA. It's okay to ask for help, and at this stage of the problem, you have clear questions you can ask.

Asking for Help

When you ask for help, be sure to present the facts. Even if those facts involve you messing up. What happened, then what you did, and where you are now. Be ready with all the solutions you've tried, and don't be put off if they tell you to try the same thing, but slightly differently.

I DID SOMETHING WRONG AND I DON'T KNOW WHAT TO DO NOW

The fact that you know you did something wrong is a pretty good sign. Assuming no one is hurt, nothing illegal or unethical has occurred, and we are just talking about a run-of-the-mill whoops, we can move on to what I like to call a post-whoops analysis.

A post-whoops analysis is an opportunity for you to learn from past incidents. It's based on a postmortem analysis, but instead of a discussion, I prefer to do these privately. The idea is to do this with a blame-free mindset and be as objective as you can be.

> "The function of an expert is not to be more right than other people, but to be wrong for more sophisticated reasons."
>
> –**David Butler**, as cited in Bryden (1986)

🔆 TOOL 12.3:   POST-WHOOPS ANALYSIS

Instructions: Fill out your responses to the questions below. Be as honest as possible. The worksheet can't judge you.

- What happened?

_____

_____

_____

_____

- Who, What, When, Where, Why?

_____

_____

_____

- What actions were taken? Which were effective? Which were detrimental?

_____

_____

- Plot the series of events in a timeline format. Be as detailed as possible.

$$\longleftarrow \longrightarrow$$

- What went well? What didn't go well? How could you prevent this issue from happening again?

When I was in my first year of being a BCBA, I ended up making an insane mistake, twice. I was working with the adult population when I was told that my client was going into hospice. This isn't something that's uncommon in that population, and you should be prepared for it. Well, I didn't know what hospice was. I had been lucky enough not to have firsthand experience with end-of-life care at that point. I used context clues and the presence of a grief expert to piece together that the client had died (that is not what happened). I told my supervisor that my client had died, and we started the process to terminate services, after getting together to share memories as a team. The next week I got a video call from my supervisor and the client—he was very much alive and was amused. I was overjoyed but also very embarrassed. This managed to happen one more time—my lesson was not learned. I told this same supervisor that he passed *again*. This time he just wasn't in the house when I went, so of course I thought he had died. It seemed rude to ask and make all the home staff feel sad, so I didn't confirm before telling my supervisor. He in fact had not died and arrived back home while I was there with the same supervisor, meeting with another client in the same house. The fact that I survived my first year is a testament to that supervisor's patience.

SURVIVAL BASICS

If you don't know what to do, you aren't alone. Reach out to whomever you can, and don't be afraid to pick yourself back up.

- Remember the tally sheet cannot miraculously tell you the answer, no matter how long you stare at it. If there isn't an active emergency or present danger, switch gears and come back to it later.

- Practice turning your question into more, or at least different, questions.

- You can't do all of the things all of the time.

- Journals are your friend. Even if you feel like strangers now, get to know them, spend some time together, and you'll soon be inseparable.

- When everything is terrible, make sure you have taken care of you: water, food, rest, repeat.

- Remember to follow up mistakes with a post-whoops analysis to make it a learning experience instead of a shameful one.

CHAPTER 13

Beating Burnout

This chapter was one of the hardest for me to write, and one of the first chapter ideas I had. I've had an on-again, off-again relationship with *burnout* for my entire clinical career. I have a bit of an all-or-nothing personality (emphasis on *all*), with a healthy dose of FOMO (fear of missing out). This combination has given me ambition and a decent amount of productivity, but no ability to "pump the brakes." Early in my career when I was complaining about a heavy workload, I was told that I was responsible for setting my own boundaries. I look back on that conversation often; the advice was sound, but I did not have the skill set to say no to myself, let alone anyone else.

Work stress combined with personal stressors was more than I could cope with. It began to impact my physical health, and pumping the brakes was no longer a choice. I know that my experience isn't uncommon. In a survey of over 800 ABA practitioners actively providing services, from students to BCBA-D's, 72% reported medium to high levels of burnout (Slowiak & DeLongchamp, 2022). Burnout is pervasive in our field, so it's something every behavior analyst should be aware of.

According to the World Health Organization (WHO), burnout (or occupational burnout) is a syndrome resulting from chronic work-related stress, with symptoms characterized by "feelings of energy depletion or exhaustion; increased mental distance from one's job, or feelings of negativism or cynicism related to one's job; and reduced professional efficacy" (WHO, 2019, para. 4).

It should be noted that while the WHO defines burnout, it does not classify it as a medical/mental health condition. Nor is it outlined in the *DSM-5-TR*, which is the current *DSM* at the writing of this chapter (American Psychiatric Association, 2022).

🎯 EXERCISE 13.1:   REFLECTING ON BURNOUT

What has been your experience with burnout?

How would you define burnout based on the topography (what it looks like)?

HISTORY OF BURNOUT

Now that we have a better idea of what burnout is, let's talk about where our current understanding of burnout comes from.

Figure 13.1: Burnout Evolution

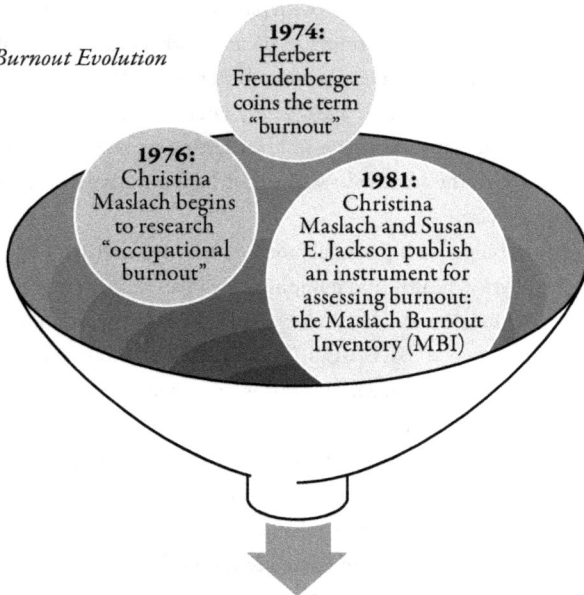

1974: Herbert Freudenberger coins the term "burnout"

1976: Christina Maslach begins to research "occupational burnout"

1981: Christina Maslach and Susan E. Jackson publish an instrument for assessing burnout: the Maslach Burnout Inventory (MBI)

As of **2018**, nine countries recognize occupational burnout to be a medical disorder.

(Lastovkova et al., 2018; Schaufeli, 2017)

Herbert Freudenberger is credited with coining the term "burnout" in 1974, although the term "vocational burnout" was used to describe air traffic controllers a few years earlier (Samra, 2018). Freudenberger linked burnout with the "caring professions" such as education and healthcare (Freudenberger, 1974). Christina Maslach began her research in occupational burnout that spanned decades shortly after, in 1976. Maslach also noted a connection with the caring professions and interesting gender correlations between individuals likely to report experiencing burnout. Evolving research at the writing of this chapter asserts that task complexity and low resources in the work environment may also play a factor in developing burnout (Müller-Leonhardt et al., 2014).

BURNOUT CHECK

If you have concerns that you may be experiencing burnout, I recommend reviewing the Maslach Burnout Inventory (MBI) self-assessment tool. It is available for purchase, or your primary care/mental health provider may be able to provide it to you.

Below is a "temperature check" inspired by the MBI. It isn't a substitute for the MBI or intended for any clinical use. Respond to the questions in the section below and fill out the thermometer. Be sure to use a different color for each section score on your thermometer (for easy direct comparison).

⊚ EXERCISE 13.2:   BURNOUT TEMPERATURE CHECK

Take a moment to check in with yourself and answer the questions below.

Yes / No   **Emotionally Exhausted**

☐   ☐   I work too hard.

☐   ☐   I feel undervalued at work.

☐   ☐   I feel like I can't take on anything else at work or I'm going to lose it.

☐   ☐   I feel drained when I finish work on a regular basis.

Yes / No   **Depersonalization**

☐   ☐   I feel tired when I wake up in the morning.

☐   ☐   I feel like I am harsher to my coworkers or clients than I am to people in my personal life.

☐   ☐   I feel like my coworkers or clients make me responsible for their problems.

☐   ☐   I worry that I am starting to no longer care about my work.

Yes / No   **Personal Achievement**

☐   ☐   In my work, I do not feel I can handle things calmly.

☐   ☐   I find it difficult to, or I am not able to, create a relaxing environment at work.

☐   ☐   I do not feel close to my coworkers or clients.

☐   ☐   I do not feel I have accomplished something worthwhile in my job.

Add your scores for each section below. Remember this is not a clinical tool; it's just a way to check in with yourself. I've added a few extra lines so that you can keep checking in with yourself. Each "yes" is equal to 1 point. Here are my scores as an example:

Emotionally Exhausted	Depersonalization	Personal Achievement	Total
2	1	3	6

Emotionally Exhausted	Depersonalization	Personal Achievement	Total

Now take those scores and put them into the thermometer.   (Here's my example:)

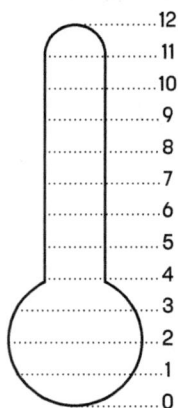

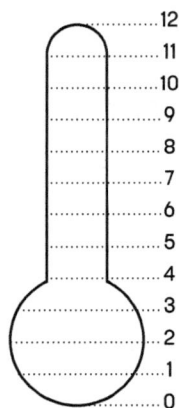

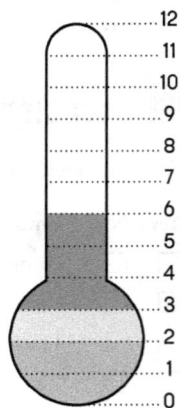

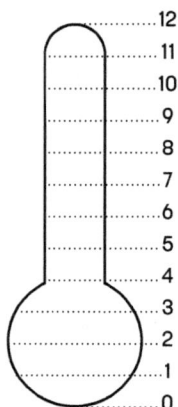

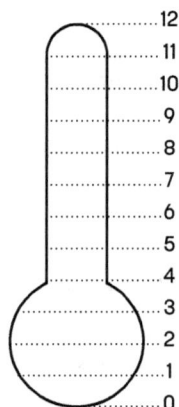

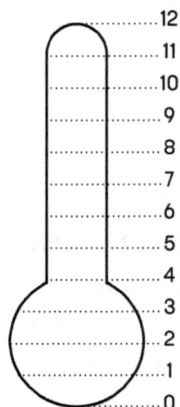

Emotionally Exhausted

With emotional exhaustion, you may begin to notice that weekends are no longer long enough to recharge.

Depersonalization

With depersonalization, you detach from relationships. You may notice an increase in cynical feelings. I tend to experience depersonalization first; it's the first indicator for me that something "isn't right." Compassion fatigue is another name for this sensation.

Lack of Personal Achievement

Experiencing a lack of personal achievement may leave you feeling that nothing you do matters. When this sensation comes over you, take some time to review graphs and treatment planning. I've found it gives some objectivity to the fact that what we do matters.

Burnout Roundup

Now that you've seen my scores, I want you to know they weren't always like that. There were times where I would have maxed out that temperature check. Early in my career I was learning to supervise, doing all of my own direct, and experiencing the symptoms of an autoimmune condition I didn't understand. At that time, I had four direct early intervention clients I supervised (around 8 hours per week); I had 12 adult clients (a good amount of that was consulting, so let's say 6 hours per week); I was doing direct on about four cases (8 hours per week); and 12 hours of unpaid drive time a week (that's rural life for you). Then, factor in caregiver training, treatment planning, graphing, material making, and invoicing to round out the week (all but caregiver training was unpaid). It doesn't seem too bad on paper (or maybe it does!), but my stress was through the roof—I felt overworked and broke. Learning how to manage a caseload with a wide variety of client types and expectations was a lot. I was in the phase of growth where I had to write reports two or three times to get them right. I was completely burnt out to the point where it probably wasn't super fun to be my coworker. I knew I had to cut out stress, but I didn't know how.

THE "HOW" I WISH I KNEW THEN

Being a behavior analyst can be is stressful, but that doesn't mean we can't do anything about it. I learned to use three "-izes" to survive a stressful role—assuming a trip to the beach isn't an option.

- Categorize
- Organize
- Prioritize

Categorize

This method for task categorization was created by former president Dwight D. Eisenhower in 1954 and is appropriately named the Eisenhower matrix (Allen et al., 2021).

Figure 13.2: *Eisenhower Matrix*

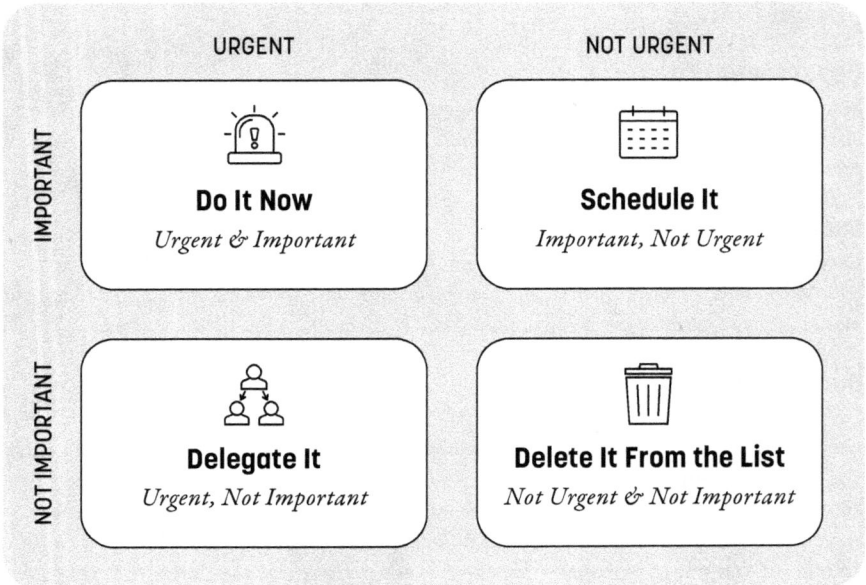

How do you define important?
- Will it impact other people if not completed?
- Are other tasks dependent on this one?

How do you define urgent?
- Is it overdue?
- Is it almost due?
- Are there immediate consequences if it does not get done?

Learn to sort things into those blocks (and not just put everything into the Urgent & Important column). That makes you a Hair-On-Fire Human. I've been there and done that, so you don't have to.

⊚ EXERCISE 13.3:   SORT YOUR TO-DO LIST

Take a moment to sort your work to-do list into these categories. If you have more than three in the Urgent & Important category, try again.

Urgent & Important

Important But Not Urgent

Urgent But Not Important

Not Important & Not Urgent

This is one way I categorize tasks. Another is by the level of concentration required and the location I need to do them. For example, I need privacy and peace for treatment planning and graphing—so my options are home or the office. Responding to emails and building Excel templates don't require privacy, so I can be more flexible on location, but they still require a level of concentration. There are no charts for this one, but think about all the spaces you work in and identify which one gives you your best work.

Organize

I've noticed a direct connection between my space and my stress. I am the queen of procrastination cleaning.

What organization is:
- Knowing where to find what you need.
- Knowing what you need to complete a task.
- Knowing you have a task to complete.
- Giving yourself enough time to complete a task.

What organization is not:
- Scrubbing a 2,000-square-foot clinic to avoid writing a treatment plan. Yes, I did that. No, it did not fix my problem.
- Packing your schedule to the brim.

As clinicians, we have a lot to manage. Don't forget to manage yourself with the same care and kindness that you manage your clients and stakeholders with. You are the most important client. If you wouldn't do it to someone else, don't do it to yourself.

When you're ready to organize, here are some tips to get you started.

- Set calendar events for important items like treatment plans. I like to set mine a week in advance. That way I have built-in time to prepare.
  - At one company I worked for, it was common practice to use calendar invites—it's where I learned the trick. When I was in my first or second year, I forgot to hit

"accept" on an invite, and because I had no master spreadsheet to remind me, we ran 5 months over authorization (meaning the treatment plan was past due and we stopped getting paid for 5 months) before anyone caught it.

- Keep a central file. This means one file for everything you need, and one place to look when you need something. I use a spreadsheet linked with a cloud-like software, so I can see it from a computer or phone. The spreadsheet has pages with deadlines, to-do lists, and anything specific I need to keep track of. I also put personal items on the list, so I don't schedule work appointments on top of personal ones.

- Build in breaks when you make your daily schedule.
  ◦ When the world starts to feel like it's closing in, answer these questions:
    - Have I eaten?
    - Have I had water in the last 2 hours?
    - Have I taken a breathing break?
  ◦ If the answer is "no" to any of the above, do at least two on the list before attempting your next task.

- Keep notes on supervision sessions and clients. You won't remember everything, and most company supervision forms won't be detailed enough to record everything you discuss and all your action items. Always follow any applicable HIPAA/privacy guidelines!

- Organize your in-person spaces the same way you organize your digital spaces, or vice versa. Pick one system and apply it to *everything*.

- Label all of your files the same way. If you color-code, keep a consistent system.
  ◦ I once changed my color coding system because I forgot my markers that day. I'm embarrassed to admit how much it messed with my head. Learn from me.

- Don't fight your natural tendencies—as Aubrey Daniels says, "behavior goes where reinforcement flows" (Daniels, 2007).
  ◦ I used to always leave my keys in the sink. Some may call it a fun quirk; others may call it a nuisance. I tried everything to change this behavior: I put cute "reinforcing" key hooks by the door. I CLEARED OUT my preferred red-and-white store—the one that rhymes with Margaret. I finally took a second to think about why it was happening. At the time, I was working in a clinic. I would come home, immediately wash my hands, and then change from my work clothes to my home clothes—it all made sense! My keys now live in a cute tray *next to* the sink. As long as I know where they are, it works.

- Clean out your car, especially if you do home-based services. You'll feel better—trust me. (I'm still finding DTT cards under my car seats—don't be like me).

- Organize your emails. File responses by content, not by the sender, into individual files. When I was in the clinical field, one of my mentors taught me to do this by client. That way, if I needed "receipts" I could pull up the file and see everything I had. I've now applied this to all my emails.

○ Delete the junk: all of the ads solicitations, or irrelevant emails. That said, you don't want to delete emails that have clinical content or emails that will come up again later (e.g., cancelations, policy updates, etc.).

Prioritize

You Get Three
Pick three things to accomplish in a day. I suggest pulling them from the Urgent & Important category. As you get your sea legs this year, you'll notice that the more proactive you are, the less you have in this category. I'm not saying when someone comes in needing your help in an emergency you say, "Sorry, I've hit my three." No, don't be that guy. When it comes to your *own* priorities for the day, that's when you pick three.

Worst Thing First
Do the thing you are dreading first. Everything else will be easy, and you can ride the satisfaction train to the relaxation station. That was lame, but doing the worst thing first isn't.

When Everything Is Urgent, Nothing Is
I was working a clinical position, and I was covering a 4-hour direct therapy session with a child. In those 4 hours, I received 18 emails, several messages through an internal messaging system, and three texts saying something along the lines of, "Did you see my email/internal message?" Out of those emails, only about two were urgent, and both of those individuals had all the same information I did, so whether I was actually needed was debatable. I wanted to pull out my hair that day, and as a result I stopped reacting so much.

To help illustrate the point, there is a phenomenon among clinical nurses called *alarm fatigue*. It is essentially a sensory overload that occurs when a nurse is exposed to too many alarms. When they hear constant alarms, they stop reacting to them, and sometimes this impacts clinical care because they miss an important alarm (Woo & Bacon, 2020).

EXERCISE 13.4: CHECK YOUR ALARMS

What "alarms" go off during your day?

Are you at risk for alarm fatigue? If so, what "alarms" can you get rid of?

SURVIVAL BASICS

I have also been the other person in the "when everything is urgent, nothing is" story. I have been the Hair-On-Fire Human. As you learn to prioritize your own time and energy, remember to extend the courtesy to those around you. In your first year, you'll see a lot of great people who want to help you learn to do great things. Be sure to respect their time and not be a Hair-On-Fire Human.

CHAPTER 14

Lay of the Land: ABA Across Settings

Like many of you, I did most of my training in a clinic-based setting and worked primarily with young children with developmental delays/autism spectrum disorder (ASD). I'd just about completed my field experience hours before I saw a community-based instruction treatment model. I'd been a BCBA for a year before I had the opportunity to work with an adult client, and there are many settings I've yet to gain any firsthand experience in. Each new setting changed my perspective and application of the science. On top of those benefits, changing settings helped me stay in the field. When I felt "singed around the edges," with burnout on its way, I moved out of direct clinical service and was able to continue on in the field through working in higher education.

When preparing this chapter, I overheard a new BCBA say, "I wish someone would have just given me a lay of the land, so I knew what my options were." I'd thought the same thing as a new BCBA, and so here we are. Grab your passports and travel bag—we are going through just a few of the "lands" in the ABA "World." We will cover languages spoken, can't-miss landmarks (subspecialties), and notable exports (follow-up materials for you to check out). In a few of our "lands," we have interviews with locals to give you advice for your visit. See *Figure 14.1: ABA World* on the following page.

Figure 14.1: ABA World

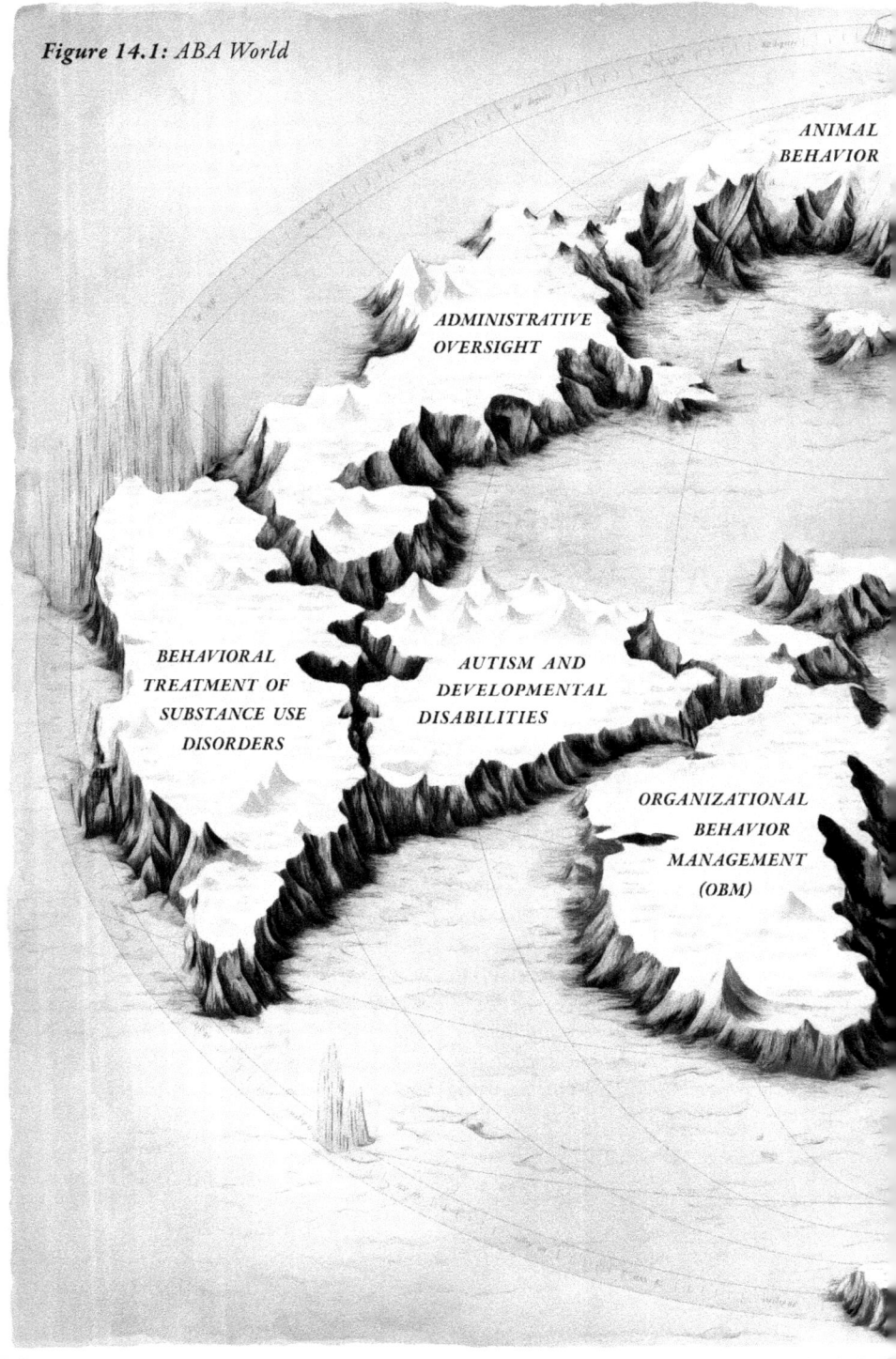

ANIMAL
BEHAVIOR

ADMINISTRATIVE
OVERSIGHT

BEHAVIORAL
TREATMENT OF
SUBSTANCE USE
DISORDERS

AUTISM AND
DEVELOPMENTAL
DISABILITIES

ORGANIZATIONAL
BEHAVIOR
MANAGEMENT
(OBM)

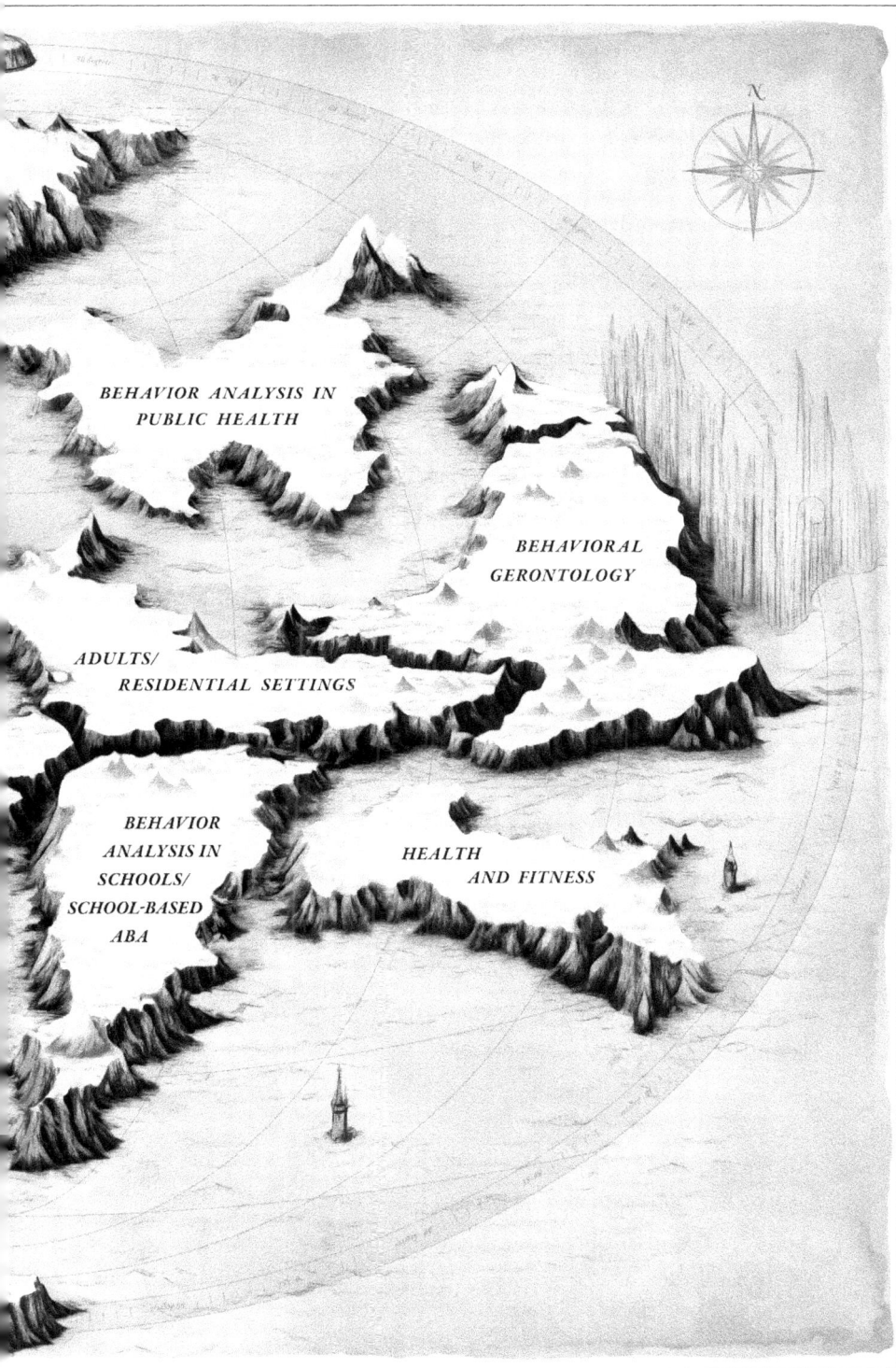

BEHAVIOR ANALYSIS IN
PUBLIC HEALTH

BEHAVIORAL
GERONTOLOGY

ADULTS/
RESIDENTIAL SETTINGS

BEHAVIOR
ANALYSIS IN
SCHOOLS/
SCHOOL-BASED
ABA

HEALTH
AND FITNESS

Autism and Developmental Disabilities

General Overview: BCBAs here work with individuals with ASD or other developmental disabilities, usually directly, to reduce maladaptive behavior and increase skills. These interventions can take place in homes, schools, community-based settings, or clinics.

Languages Spoken: ABA, Insurance, Corporate-light

Can't-Miss Landmarks (Subspecialties):

- Early Intervention
- Severe Maladaptive/Dangerous Behavior Reduction
- Sleep Support
- Feeding

Notable Exports:

Harris and Weiss (2007): *Right from the Start: Behavioral Intervention for Young Children with Autism*

LeBlanc and Gillis (2012): "Behavioral Interventions for Children with Autism Spectrum Disorders"

Maurice et al. (1996): *Behavioral Intervention for Young Children with Autism: A Manual for Parents and Professionals*

Behavior Analysis in Schools/School-Based ABA

General Overview: BCBAs here look to improve learning and teaching. These BCBAs can be found in many different types of schools, and across grade levels. They often act in the role of consultant.

Languages Spoken: ABA, IEP, Group Contingency-ese, Government-ese (DOE dialect)

Can't-Miss Landmarks (Subspecialties):

- Classroom Management
- Curriculum and Instruction
- Evidence-Based Education
- General, Gifted, Mainstream, and Special Education
- Instructional Design
- Personalized System of Instruction
- Precision Teaching

- School-Wide Positive Behavior Support
- Systems of Schooling (Administration, Policy)
- Teacher Education

Notable Exports:
Barrish et al. (1969): "Good Behavior Game: Effects of Individual Contingencies for Group Consequences on Disruptive Behavior in a Classroom"

Heward et al. (2005): *Focus on Behavior Analysis in Education: Achievements, Challenges, and Opportunities*

Keller (1968): "Good-Bye, Teacher ..."

INTERVIEW WITH A LOCAL

Meet Amber S.: Amber S. received her BS in Psychology from Francis Marion University in 2016 and her MS in Applied Behavior Analysis from Florida State University in 2018. She has 6 years of clinical experience providing behavior-analytic services to individuals with developmental disabilities and other diagnoses in schools, homes, and community settings. Amber's primary clinical experience is in the treatment of language and social skills delays associated with ASD.

✦   ✦   ✦

How Amber S. describes her work: *"As a school consultant, I worked in schools to evaluate students in classrooms when a behavior plan or functional behavior assessment was requested by the school. I trained teachers and staff how to properly implement the strategies in the FBA and behavior plan and how to take data on the student's progress. I also graphed and analyzed that data and then presented to school administration to provide recommendations on any modifications that could be made to a classroom to promote success with the goals from the student's behavior plan."*

What drew Amber S. to schools: *"I enjoyed being able to focus more of my work on a 'big picture' approach. I loved working hands-on with kids, but it was an added challenge to train others to do what I would do."*

What skills and traits Amber S. says are vital to "survival" in schools: *"Rapport-building. It's not enough to know the science and to know what should be done, because at the end of the day you're training someone else to do the things you would do. And absolutely nothing will get done if you don't have a good working relationship with school staff and the teachers."*

Amber S.'s advice if you want to begin working in schools: *"My biggest struggle when starting out in school consulting was gaining enough rapport with the teachers. I felt like I needed to wear the BCBA hat all the time, and that caused some friction when the teachers did not want to talk behavior all the time. Remember to be a human and treat the school staff like they're humans too. You can be funny and show the side of you that's not a clinician. I often earned more respect from everyone that way."*

Health and Fitness

General Overview: These behavior analysts work directly with individuals (usually outside of a larger health system) to improve health and wellness outcomes. Behavior analysts in these settings may work as consultants and work directly with clients. Knowledge of health, wellness, and nutrition may be required.

Languages Spoken: ABA, Gym

Can't-Miss Landmarks (Subspecialties):
- Nutrition Coaching
- Health Promotion
- Behavioral Health Coaching

Notable Exports:
Kurti and Dallery (2013): "Internet-Based Contingency Management Increases Walking in Sedentary Adults"

Normand et al. (2015): "Applied Behavior Analysis for Health and Fitness"

Petry et al. (2011): "A Low-Cost Reinforcement Procedure Improves Short-Term Weight Loss Outcomes"

Behavioral Treatment of Substance Use Disorders

General Overview: BCBAs here often work in medical and academic research. They may also be in specialty care clinics, or at the Veterans Affairs (VA) clinics. These BCBAs work closely with prescribing physicians in multidisciplinary panels. Additional knowledge of substance abuse may be required.

Languages Spoken: ABA, Research-ese, Acceptance and Commitment Therapy (ACT)

Can't-Miss Landmarks (Subspecialties):
- Acceptance and Commitment Therapy
- Relapse Prevention

Notable Exports:
Godley et al. (2014): "The Adolescent Community Reinforcement Approach (A-CRA) as a Model Paradigm for the Management of Adolescents with Substance Use Disorders and Co-Occurring Psychiatric Disorders"

Gupta (2015): "Contingency Management: Why It Pays to Quit"

Higgins et al. (2008): *Contingency Management in Substance Abuse Treatment*

Behavior Analysis in Public Health

General Overview: BCBAs here look at "big picture" trends in behavior. Public health often has a behavior component, and this is where the BCBA comes in. BCBAs here may work for larger organizations that focus on public health (e.g., the CDC).

Languages Spoken: ABA, Research-ese, Statistics-light, Government-ish

Can't-Miss Landmarks (Subspecialties):
- The Three Levels of Public Health
  - Prevention
  - Screening
  - Treatment

Notable Exports:
Horne et al. (2004): "Increasing Children's Fruit and Vegetable Consumption: A Peer-Modelling and Rewards-Based Intervention"

Hovell et al. (2002): "The Behavioral Ecological Model: Integrating Public Health and Behavioral Science"

Normand et al. (2021): "Leveraging Applied Behavior Analysis Research and Practice in the Service of Public Health"

Organizational Behavior Management (OBM)

General Overview: Organizational behavior management (OBM) improves employee performance through the assessment of and modifications to the working environment. BCBAs who work in OBM are likely to be consultants and may work in firms with other consultants or "in-house," meaning they are employed directly by the organization for which they provide OBM services. Those in OBM often travel in disguise; their titles don't always give away that they belong to the greater ABA World.

Languages Spoken: ABA, Corporate, Statistics-light

Can't-Miss Landmarks (Subspecialties):
- Performance Management
- Behavior-Based Safety
- Behavioral Systems Analysis
- Consumer Behavior Analysis
- Health and Wellness

- Monetary Incentive Systems
- Training and Development
- Leadership and Culture

Notable Exports:
Daniels (2000): *Bringing Out the Best in People: How to Apply the Astonishing Power of Positive Reinforcement*

Daniels and Bailey (2014): *Performance Management: Changing Behavior that Drives Organizational Effectiveness*

McSween and Hockman (in press): *The New Values-Based Safety: Using Behavioral Science to Improve Your Safety Culture*

INTERVIEW WITH A LOCAL

This local has chosen to keep her name private due to the sensitive nature of her work. We will call her Ashley K.

Meet Ashley K.: Ashley worked in the autism arena for the first half of her career. She worked primarily in clinics and in homes for just short of a decade before she sought a new challenge and set her sights on making the move to OBM.

✦   ✦   ✦

How Ashley K. describes her work: *"I serve as an analyst for a defense contractor and my responsibilities are mainly focused on increasing appropriate, ethical behaviors of employees and reducing risk in areas that could damage the company (either their reputation, their standing with the government, or pose a risk of major fines from the government). This includes acting as a consultant for security and threat assessment groups. My primary job is to analyze the current data of performance metrics the company wants to see and provide recommendations based on what the data describe in order to improve the company as a whole in regard to ethical behavior and limiting risk to the company."*

What drew Ashley K. to OBM: *"I wanted to get out of clinical work. I loved working with kids but unfortunately suffered pretty severe burnout and I wanted to challenge myself by doing more OBM work."*

What skills and traits Ashley K. says are vital to "survival" in OBM: *"A huge recommendation would be to get familiar with analyzing data on a large scale. Huge companies will have LOTS of data and a simple Excel table won't always be appropriate. Power BI and Tableau will allow you to present a lot of data in a very succinct way. Additionally, get comfortable with 'translating' ABA into terms that other people will understand. Your skills as a BCBA are VERY valuable to other industries, but the problem is that our field looks so specialized when looking at a resume or your work experience. Be able to explain how your knowledge helps the business do their job better and speak to how humans behave and learn."*

Ashley K.'s advice if you want to begin working in OBM: *"Take a data analytics course. As a BCBA you already know how to analyze data, but this will teach you how to do so in a way that a business will value."*

Behavioral Gerontology

General Overview: BCBAs here apply the principles of behavior to age-related concerns. BCBAs can work directly with seniors or with their caregivers to provide treatment. They may also work in coordination with multidisciplinary panels (e.g., prescribing physicians, speech therapists, OTs).

Languages Spoken: ABA, Pharmacology (Awareness dialect)

Can't-Miss Landmarks (Subspecialties):
- Neurocognitive Disorders
- Memory Problems
- Behavioral Medicine
- Health and Fitness

Notable Exports:
Drossel and Trahan (2015): "Behavioral Interventions are First-Line Treatments for Managing Changes Associated with Cognitive Decline"

Fisher et al. (2000): "Behavioral Interventions for Patients with Dementia"

LeBlanc et al. (2011): "Behavioral Gerontology"

Animal Behavior

General Overview: BCBAs work with animal trainers and caregivers to develop skills, usually related to tolerating medical care, teaching functional skills, and reducing maladaptive behavior. Having background knowledge and species-specific knowledge may be required. There is a long-standing connection between applied behavior analysis and work with animals in laboratory or applied settings.

Languages Spoken: ABA, Animal Lover-ese, but still requires fluency in People-ese

Can't-Miss Landmarks (Subspecialties):
- Animal Husbandry
- Environmental Enrichment
- Animal Health and Wellness

Notable Exports:
Dorey et al. (2009): "Functional Analysis and Treatment of Self-Injury in a Captive Olive Baboon"

Martin et al. (2011): "Functional Analysis and Treatment of Human-Directed Undesirable Behavior by a Captive Chimpanzee"

Poling et al. (2010): "Using Giant African Pouched Rats to Detect Tuberculosis in Human Sputum Samples: 2009 Findings"

INTERVIEW WITH A LOCAL

Meet Cassie V.M.: Cassie's past professional experience includes 9 years working in zoological facilities. She received extensive training in animal husbandry, environmental enrichment, animal training, and education. Through working in zoological facilities with animals, Cassie learned about the science of behavior and has been fascinated ever since. She is a graduate of the Applied Behavior Analysis and Organizational Behavior Management master's program at the Florida Institute of Technology. While in graduate school, Cassie had the privilege of learning from the team at ABA Technologies, Inc., about curriculum and instructional design. This experience ignited her passion for the teaching and dissemination of behavior analysis. Cassie is currently an Instructional Design Specialist.

✦   ✦   ✦

How Cassie V.M. describes her work: *"A behavior analyst working in zoological facilities would contribute to animal training and environmental enrichment initiatives such as behavior management plans, behavior evaluations, and staff training programs related to the science of behavior. For example, a behavior analyst may assist animal care teams in implementing environmental enrichment to promote species-typical behavior. Additionally, a behavior analyst may assist in the training of husbandry or medical-related behaviors such as voluntary blood draws or nail trims that would provide the animal the opportunity to participate in their own healthcare."*

What drew Cassie V.M. to zoological facilities: *"My passion for animals led me to this setting. My past professional experience includes 9 years working in zoological facilities. Through working in zoological facilities with animals, I learned about the science of behavior. After receiving my master's degree, I was able to combine my behavior-analytic education and my prior animal-related experience to assist animal care teams in reaching behavior-change goals."*

What skills and traits Cassie V.M. says are vital to "survival" in zoological facilities: *"Collaboration is a skill that is vital to working in this setting. There are often multiple professionals from a variety of disciplines who assist in the care of the animals. It is imperative that a behavior analyst working in this setting be accommodating of the other professionals while also ensuring their recommended behavior-change plan is achievable and successful."*

Cassie V.M.'s advice if you want to begin working in zoological facilities: *"My advice for new behavior analysts wanting to work in this setting is to gain experience in zoological facilities. Volunteering and seeking mentorship are some great ways to get involved. My experience caring for animals was immensely helpful when applying for behavior-analytic positions in the animal field, as it provided credibility and a background in animal care."*

For the last part of this trip around the ABA World, I leave you in the very capable hands of Thomas Freeman to share about two final areas.

MEET THE LOCAL

Thomas Freeman, MS, BCBA, began working in behavior analysis in 1979 at the Fernald State School, a large state residential institution in Massachusetts. He moved to Florida in 1995, earned an MS in ABA in 2000 at Florida Institute of Technology, and became a BCBA in 2001. He was licensed as a behavior analyst in the State of New York in 2016, and in 2017 was licensed in Massachusetts. In addition to over 4 decades of experience in ABA, he has helped conduct a variety of studies in wild animal behavior research, including work with North Pacific Humpback Whales, Hawaiian Spinner Dolphins, and Orangutans in Borneo. Currently, he is the Senior Vice President at ABA Technologies, Inc., where he helps teach and create course materials for the online program in behavior analysis at Florida Institute of Technology. Prior to his current position, he served for 10 years as a District Behavior Analyst for the State of Florida's Agency for Persons with Disabilities, providing oversight of all behavioral services across two counties. Thomas has produced a variety of presentations and publications, including co-authorship of the chapter "Ethical and Professional Responsibilities of Applied Behavior Analysts" in *Applied Behavior Analysis* (Cooper et al., 2020) and a chapter on "Grief and Developmental Disabilities: Considerations for Disenfranchised Populations" in the *Handbook of Social Justice in Loss and Grief* (Harris & Bordere, 2016).

✦   ✦   ✦

WORKING WITH ADULTS IN RESIDENTIAL SETTINGS

"Upon leaving graduate school, many behavior analysts find immediate work in early intervention programs providing services to children diagnosed with ASD. However, a significant need continues to exist for BCBAs and Board Certified Assistant Behavior Analysts® (BCaBA®s) under supervision in adult residential facilities, where individuals are typically diagnosed with an intellectual disability (ID), and who often display a psychiatric or other medical comorbidity. These individuals exhibit a variety of functional skill deficits and may exhibit significant problem behaviors as well (e.g., assault, self-injury, property destruction, inappropriate social behaviors). Many of these individuals receive services from professionals in various disciplines (medical, dental, physical/occupational/speech therapy, vocational training) and often receive medication management services from either a psychiatrist or a neurologist. Staff persons in these settings tend to be high school graduates at best and working for relatively low wages in a difficult environment. Turnover rates can be very high.

"Probably the most challenging aspect when you begin this work is how different it can be in comparison to what one has read about or even experienced in a graduate program, especially if one's supervised experience was in a clinical setting connected to that graduate program, where many graduate students and experienced supervisors provided ABA services to nonresidential clients (especially children). By contrast, in the community,

resources are typically very limited and the behavior analyst, usually the only person trained in ABA in that setting, must not only find a way to provide adequate staff training for consistent program implementation and data collection, but must also ensure adequate monitoring and feedback systems, while providing leadership that inspires confidence and eventual dedication to the behavioral approach.

Behavior analysts must rely on the concepts and principles of our science to succeed, including the use of differential reinforcement, successive approximations, shaping and fading, and pairing. For example, if the behavior analyst can quickly solve a few simple problems that have long plagued the staff (reducing client toilet accidents for example), the staff begin to pair the presence of the behavior analyst with the reduction of aversive events in their environment. If collection of unnecessary/unutilized data has been required before your arrival, get rid of it! If staff persons see the behavior analyst pitching in and helping wherever needed (at meals for example), especially where program implementation is involved, the BCBA builds credibility and trust. The behavior analyst becomes paired with negative reinforcement—aversive aspects of the environment are reduced when they are around—and if the BCBA is supportive and finds things to praise, the BCBA becomes an S^D for both positive and negative reinforcing events. Moreover, the BCBA should focus on leading an open and nonthreatening team process, where everyone is encouraged to speak up in regular staff meetings and data reviews. Focus on giving people credit for their suggestions (even if you guided them into making that suggestion), and soon they will begin to take real ownership of program success. It is amazing what success can follow when you stop needing to take the credit for a good idea and instead are always on the lookout for opportunities to give credit to others.

Finally, the behavior analyst should seek to work collaboratively with other professionals in an interdisciplinary team process, subtly working to integrate the behavioral approach into all services. This is especially important when working in psychotropic medication management. The best way for a behavior analyst to earn the confidence of the prescribing physician is to initially offer the physician help in gathering whatever information (data-based and quantified) the physician wants—essentially to become their eyes and ears in the residential environment—which assists them in making better informed medication management decisions. This will build a professional trust relationship over time that will eventually provide many benefits in coordinating medication and behavioral services for the best interest of the client. Without this approach, the doctors are likely to brusquely ask you why you are attending a medication management meeting, and to please leave."

✦   ✦   ✦

PROVIDING ADMINISTRATIVE OVERSIGHT FOR A STATE AGENCY OR PRIVATE PROVIDER

"Sometime later in your career, after you have gained significant experience in the field, you may have the opportunity to serve in an administrative capacity, wherein you provide oversight of behavior analysis services provided by other behavior analysts. You should strongly consider taking such a position, especially if you have provided clinical services for several years. Younger behavior analysts can greatly benefit from your experience and

careful guidance, and the professional model you can provide. This also offers you the opportunity to act as a liaison with funding sources and other supports necessary for the delivery of behavioral services, and to possibly have input on policy decisions relating to the broad delivery of our services.

When in such a position, consider your role very carefully. You are not a supervisor. You are an administrator. You must model a professional, ethical approach and dedication to excellence. Administrative oversight is often a regulatory requirement in a state or other jurisdiction. You must provide clear guidance as to what is expected of the service providers. But, as with all behavior analysis services, we must rely on the concepts and principles of our science. Differential reinforcement works wonders with individuals who have had limited oversight in the past, as does the use of shaping, fading, and timely feedback. Using reinforcement of successive approximations can result in improved performance by the individuals over whom you have administrative authority. Sometimes you may even use behavior skills training for certain groups of providers. On the other hand, reliance on harsh feedback and punishment can produce the negative side effect seen in any coercive environment. Progressive discipline should thus be viewed as your last resort and be used sparingly. Administrate with a steady, firm, but mainly reinforcing hand, and improvements in performance will, by definition, follow."

Thank you to Amber, Ashley, Cassie, and Thomas for lending their time and expertise to being the "locals" for this chapter.

🎯 EXERCISE 14.1: LOCALS

What "locals" are guiding you in your workplace?

How would you respond to the following prompts if you were a "local"?

• How would you describe your work?

- What drew you to the setting you are currently in?

- What skills are vital to that setting?

- What advice would you give to someone else?

SURVIVAL BASICS

There are so many applications of ABA; the ones here are just the tip of the iceberg. Knowing the science of human behavior and how it can be modified really can make any "land" an ABA land.

You Survived!

Congratulations—you've completed your first year! Take some time to reflect and review your "Before You Begin" journal entries at the beginning of the book and then record some memories from this last year. Your future self will thank you.

Share a struggle you had:

Share a win you had:

List some accomplishments:

What are you proud of?

What changes have you observed in yourself this year?

How have you felt about yourself?

What are you most grateful for in the last year?

Do you recognize yourself in your earlier entries?

What was the best thing you built/created?

What was the hardest lesson you learned over the past year?

What was the most humbling experience of the past year?

Share a funny story:

Share an embarrassing moment—your future self will view this more gently than you do now!

Activity Answer Keys

📝 ACTIVITY 1.1: MEETING TYPE MATCH

Instructions: As a behavior analyst, you will routinely have meetings with caregivers, members of your own team, and other service providers (more on that in Chapter 9). See if you can identify what type each meeting description might fall in.

Word bank: The Update, The Infodump, The Decider, The Boost

Caregiver/adult client meetings (external meetings):

The Infodump	Reviewing policies, procedures, and expectations
The Update	Treatment plan updates (reviewing progress)
The Decider	Client/caregiver not in compliance with policy
The Update and/or The Boost	Conducting typical caregiver training sessions
The Update and/or The Decider	A new problem behavior has occurred

Team meetings (internal meetings):

The Infodump	A policy has changed
The Update and/or The Decider	A client is engaging in new problem behavior
The Update and/or The Boost	A routine check-in about a client's progress

Meetings with other professionals (internal meetings):

The Update and/or The Decider	The client has begun a new maladaptive behavior
The Update and/or The Decider	The client is not making the expected progress
The Update	A regularly scheduled meeting about a client

Note that there is no Infodump in this section. Avoid The Infodump with other professionals unless they have invited you to share on a certain topic.

✎ ACTIVITY 1.2: SCHEDULING SUDOKU

9	8	7	3	6	5	2	1	4
3	2	5	7	4	1	8	9	6
6	1	4	8	9	2	3	7	5
1	3	6	9	8	4	7	5	2
4	9	2	5	1	7	6	8	3
5	7	8	2	3	6	1	4	9
2	4	1	6	7	9	5	3	8
7	6	3	4	5	8	9	2	1
8	5	9	1	2	3	4	6	7

✎ ACTIVITY 3.1: ASSESSMENT GRIDS

KEY	SCORE	DATE	COLOR	TESTER
1st Test	85/108	1/23/23		MA

	Domain 1	Domain 2	Domain 3	Domain 4	Domain 5	Domain 6	Domain 7	Domain 8	Domain 9
12									
11									
10									
9									
8									
7									
6									
5									
4									
3									
2									
1									

✍ ACTIVITY 4.1: CODE BREAKER

Instructions: We've spent this chapter talking a lot about codes. In the spirit of codes and cracking them, use this cryptograph to decipher one of the most commonly used codes in ABA.

Hint: CPT Code 97153

A	B	C	D	E	F	G	H	I	J	K	L	M
24		13	15		2		14	18		16		22

N	O	P	Q	R	S	T	U	V	W	X	Y	Z
9	10	21		5		17		3	1			26

A D A P T I V E
24 15 24 10 12 13 19 25

B E H A V I O R
23 25 14 24 19 18 20 21

T R E A T M E N T
12 21 25 24 12 22 25 9 12

B Y   P R O T O C O L
23 4   10 21 20 12 20 13 20 6

⚡ ACTIVITY 8.1: CLIENT CONFLICT DOS AND DON'TS

Instructions: Here are some client conflict dos and don'ts. Circle the dos and cross out the don'ts.

Communicate face-to-face

~~Assume the person doesn't understand~~

Act sooner rather than later

Be present, clear, and direct

~~Get defensive~~

~~Ignore feedback~~

Use language that is understandable (no jargon)

Understand their perspective as well as yours

~~Argue feelings~~

Focus on the present situation/problem

Manage your emotions

Recognize your differences

Actively listen

Be honest, genuine, and respectful

Be aware of body language of all parties

~~Avoid the issue~~

~~Interrupt them~~

~~Use put-downs and sarcasm~~

~~Fight about the issue on social media~~

~~Stop communication~~

✎ ACTIVITY 10.1: IEP DOS AND DON'TS

Instructions: Circle the dos and cross out the don'ts.

Bring the client's relevant records with you.

Bring the most recent graphs and behavior intervention plan (BIP).

~~Speak in jargon.~~

~~Impress all the teachers by using as many behavior-analytic words as possible.~~

Assume the school, private therapy team, and caregivers are on the same team.

~~Be defensive if nobody wants to see your BIP.~~

Be flexible and respectful of the team's time.

Read reports provided to you.

✎ ACTIVITY 10.2: IEP ACRONYM CROSSWORD

Instructions: Try your hand at the crossword below. Note that a hyphen counts as a space.

CLUES

ACROSS			DOWN	
2. ESY	4. IEP	9. LRE	1. FAPE	6. ED
3. APS	8. CBI	10. FBA	5. MTSS	7. EI

Down 1: FREE APPROPRIATE PUBLIC EDUCATION

Across 2: EXTENDED SCHOOL YEAR

Across 3: APPROVED PRIVATE SCHOOL

Across 4: INDIVIDUALIZED EDUCATION PROGRAM

Down 5: MULTI-TIERED SYSTEM OF SUPPORTS

Down 6: EMOTIONAL DISTURBANCE

Down 7: EARLY INTERVENTION

Across 8: COMMUNITY-BASED INSTRUCTION

Across 9: LEAST RESTRICTIVE ENVIRONMENT

Across 10: FUNCTIONAL BEHAVIOR ASSESSMENT

ABA Acronym Glossary

#

504: Section 504 of the Rehabilitation Act

A

AAC: Augmentative and alternative communication

AARR: Arbitrarily applicable relational responding

ABA: Applied behavior analysis

ABAI: Association for Behavior Analysis International

ABC: Autism Behavior Checklist

A-B-C: Antecedent-Behavior-Consequence

ABLLS-R: Assessment of Basic Language and Learning Skills, Revised

ACA: Affordable Care Act

ACE: Authorized Continuing Education

ACT: Acceptance and commitment therapy

ADA: Americans with Disabilities Act

AD&D: Accidental Death and Dismemberment (insurance)

ADHD: Attention-deficit/hyperactivity disorder

ADI-R: Autism Diagnostic Interview, Revised

ADOS-2: Autism Diagnostic Observation Schedule-Second Edition

ADR: Alternative dispute resolution

AFLS: Assessment of Functional Living Skills

AIT: Auditory integration training

ALJ: Administrative law judge

AO: Abolishing operation

APA: American Psychiatric Association

APBA: Association of Professional Behavior Analysts

APS: Approved private school

ASD: Autism spectrum disorder

ASE: Adverse side effect

ASL: American Sign Language

ASQ-3: Ages & Stages Questionnaires, Third Edition

ASR: Active student responding

AT: Assistive technology

B

BACB: Behavior Analyst Certification Board

BARS: Behaviorally Anchored Rating Scale

BCaBA: Board Certified Assistant Behavior Analyst

BCAT: Board Certified Autism Technician

BCBA: Board Certified Behavior Analyst

BCBA-D: Board Certified Behavior Analyst-Doctoral®

BICC: Behavioral Intervention Certification Council

BIP: Behavior intervention plan

BST: Behavioral skills training

BT: Behavior technician

C

CARS2: Childhood Autism Rating Scale, 2nd Edition

CBCL: Child Behavior Checklist

CBI: Community-based instruction

CBS: Center-based session

CDC: Centers for Disease Control and Prevention

CE: Continuing education

CEU: Continuing education unit

CHIP: Children's Health Insurance Program

CIPS: Clance Impostor Phenomenon Scale

CMO: Conditioned motivating operation

COB: Coordination of benefits

COBRA: Consolidated Omnibus Budget Reconciliation Act

CPT: Current Procedural Terminology (codes)

CRF: Continuous schedule of reinforcement

CS: Conditioned stimulus

D

DAYC-2: Developmental Assessment of Young Children, Second Edition

DD: Developmental disabilities

DDTT: Delay and denial tolerance training

DIS: Designated Instruction and Services (also Designated Instruction Services and Designated Instructional Services)

DME: Durable medical equipment

DOE: Department of Education

DOI: Digital Object Identifier

DOR: Department of Rehabilitation

DR: Differential reinforcement

DRA: Differential reinforcement of alternative behavior

DRD: Differential reinforcement of diminishing rates of responding

DREDF: Disability Rights Education & Defense Fund

DRH: Differential reinforcement of high rates of responding

DRI: Differential reinforcement of incompatible behavior

DRL: Differential reinforcement of low rates of responding

DRO: Differential reinforcement of other behavior

DRP: Differential reinforcement of paced responding

DSM: *Diagnostic and Statistical Manual of Mental Disorders*

DTT: Discrete trial training

DV: Dependent variable

DVD: Developmental verbal dyspraxia

E

EAB: Experimental analysis of behavior

EBD: Emotional behavior disturbance

ED: Emotional disturbance

EEG: Electroencephalogram

EFL: Essential for Living

EHB: Essential health benefits

EI: Early intervention

EIBI: Early intensive behavioral intervention

ELAP: Early Learning Accomplishment Profile

EO: Establishing operation

EOB: Explanation of benefits

EPSDT: Early Periodic Screening, Diagnostic and Treatment

ERP: Enterprise resource planning

ESDM: Early Start Denver Model

ESP: Early Screening Profiles

ESY: Extended school year

EXT: Extinction

F

FA: Functional analysis

FAPE: Free appropriate public education

FAST: Functional Analysis Screening Tool

FBA: Functional behavior assessment

FBI: Fluency-based instruction

FC: Facilitated communication

FCCT: Functional communication and complexity training

FCR: Functional communicative response

FCT: Functional communication training

FERPA: Family Educational Rights and Privacy Act

FI: Fixed interval

FMLA: Family and Medical Leave Act

FR: Fixed ratio

FSA: Flexible Spending Account

FT: Fixed time

FTE: Full-time equivalent

G

GARS-3: Gilliam Autism Rating Scale, Third Edition

H

HDHP: High Deductible Health Plan

HIPAA: Health Insurance Portability and Accountability Act

HMO: Health Maintenance Organization

HRA: Health Reimbursement Arrangement

HSA: Health Savings Account

I

ID: Intellectual disability

IDEA: Individuals with Disabilities Education Act

IEE: Independent educational evaluation

IEP: Individualized Education Program

IFSP: Individualized Family Service Plan

IHP: Individualized Habilitation Plan

IMR: Independent Medical Review

IOA: Interobserver agreement

IPOC: Individual Plan of Care

IPP: Individual Program Plan

IRO: Independent Review Organization

IRT: Interresponse time

IV: Independent variable

J

JABA: Journal of Applied Behavior Analysis

L

LAP: Learning Accomplishment Profile

LBA: Licensed Behavior Analyst

LCSW: Licensed Clinical Social Worker

LEA: Local Education Agency

LRE: Least restrictive environment

LTM: Least-to-most

M

MAC: Maximum Allowable Cost

M-CHAT-R: Modified Checklist for Autism in Toddlers, Revised

MEC: Minimum essential coverage

MHPAEA: Mental Health Parity and Addiction Equity Act

MO: Motivating operation

MOOP: Maximum out-of-pocket

MSDD: Mixed Specific Developmental Disorders

MSEL: Mullen Scales of Early Learning

MTL: Most-to-least

MTS: Momentary time sampling

MTSS: Multi-tiered system of supports

N

NCLB: No Child Left Behind

NET: Natural environment training

NOS: Not Otherwise Specified

NS: Neutral stimulus

NT: Neurologically typical or neurotypical

O

OAH: Office of Administrative Hearings

OBM: Organizational behavior management

OCD: Obsessive-compulsive disorder

OCR: U.S. Office for Civil Rights

ODD: Oppositional defiant disorder

OEP: Open Enrollment Period

OON: Out of network

OOP: Out-of-pocket limit or maximum

OSEP: U.S. Office of Special Education Programs

OT: Occupational therapist

P

PCORI: Patient-Centered Outcomes Research Institute

PCP: Primary care provider or physician

PDD: Pervasive developmental disorder

PDDBI: Pervasive Developmental Disorder Behavior Inventory

PDD-NOS: Pervasive Developmental Disorder-Not Otherwise Specified

PEAK: Promoting Emergence of Advanced Knowledge

PECS: Picture Exchange Communication System

PEDS: Parents' Evaluation of Development Status

PEP-3: Psychoeducational Profile, Third Edition

PHI: Protected Health Information

PIR: Partial-interval recording

PLACHECK: Planned activity check

PM: Performance management

PPN/PPO: Preferred Provider Network/ Organization

PRT: Pivotal Response Treatment

PSI-4: Parenting Stress Index, Fourth Edition

PT: Physical therapist

PTO: Paid time off

Q

QABF: Questions About Behavioral Function

R

RBT: Registered Behavior Technician

RFT: Relational frame theory

RIRD: Response interruption and redirection

Rx: Medical prescription

S

SBC: Summary of Benefits and Coverage

SCC: Standard Celeration Chart

S^D: Discriminative stimulus for reinforcement

SIB: Self-injurious behavior

SIT: Sensory integration therapy

SLP: Speech-language pathologist

SRS: Stimulus-Response-Stimulus

U

UMO: Unconditioned motivating operation

V

VA: Veterans Affairs

VB: Verbal behavior

VB-MAPP: Verbal Behavior Milestones Assessment and Placement Program

VI: Variable interval

VR: Variable ratio

VT: Variable time

W

WIR: Whole-interval recording

You're sure to encounter more acronyms in your first year and beyond. Use this page to add those other ones that come up.

Appendix:
Screenings & Assessments

ASSESSMENT	REFERENCE	WEBSITE
Ages & Stages Questionnaires	Squires, J., & Bricker, D. (2009). *Ages & Stages Questionnaires: A Parent-Completed Child Monitoring System* (3rd ed.). Brookes.	https://agesand stages.com
Ages & Stages Questionnaires: Social-Emotional	Squires, J., Bricker, D., & Twombly, E. (2015). *Ages & Stages Questionnaires: Social-Emotional: A Parent-Completed Child Monitoring System for Social-Emotional Behaviors* (2nd ed.). Brookes.	https://agesand stages.com
Assessment of Basic Language and Learning Skills, Revised	Partington, J. W. (2010). *The ABLLS-R— The Assessment of Basic Language and Learning Skills, Revised*. Behavior Analysts.	https://webablls .net
Assessment of Functional Living Skills	Partington, J. W., & Mueller, M. M. (2012). *The Assessment of Functional Living Skills guide*. Behavior Analysts.	https://parting tonbehavior analysts.com/
Autism Diagnostic Interview	Rutter, M., Le Couteur, A., & Lord, C. (2003, 2008). *Autism Diagnostic Interview, Revised*. Western Psychological Services.	https://www. wpspublish.com/
Autism Diagnostic Observation Schedule	Lord, C., Luyster, R. J., Gotham, K., & Guthrie, W. (2012). *Autism diagnostic observation schedule (ADOS-2), Part II: Toddler module* (2nd ed.). Western Psychological Services. Lord, C., Rutter, M., DiLavore, P. C., Risi, S., Gotham, K., & Bishop, S. L. (2012). *Autism diagnostic observation schedule (ADOS-2), Part 1: Modules 1–4* (2nd ed.). Western Psychological Services.	https://www.wps publish.com/
BRIGANCE Screens	French, B. (2013). *BRIGANCE Screens III technical manual*. Curriculum Associates.	https://www. curriculum associates.com/
Developmental Assessment of Young Children	Voress, J. K., & Maddox, T. (2013). *Developmental Assessment of Young Children-Second Edition*. PRO-ED.	https://www. proedinc.com/

Early Screening Profiles	Harrison, P. L. (1990). *Early Screening Profiles manual*. Pearson.	https://www.pearsonassessments.com/
Early Start Denver Model	Rogers, S. J., & Dawson, G. (2010). *Early Start Denver Model curriculum checklist for young children with autism*. The Guilford Press.	https://www.esdm.co/
Essential for Living	McGreevy, P., Fry, T., & Cornwall, C. (2012). *Essential for Living: A communication, behavior and functional skills, assessment and professional practitioner's handbook* (2nd ed.). Patrick McGreevy, Ph.D., P.A.	https://essentialforliving.com/
Functional Analysis Screening Tool	Iwata, B. A., & DeLeon, I. (1996). *The Functional Analysis Screening Tool*. The Florida Center on Self-Injury, The University of Florida. Iwata, B. A., DeLeon, I. G., & Roscoe, E. M. (2013). Reliability and validity of the Functional Analysis Screening Tool. *Journal of Applied Behavior Analysis, 46*(1), 271–284. https://doi.org/10.1002/jaba.31	https://doi.org/10.1002/jaba.31
Learning Accomplishment Profile-Diagnostic	Hardin, B. J., Peisner-Feinberg, E. S., & Weeks, S. W. (2005). *The Learning Accomplishment Profile-Diagnostic (LAP-D)· Examiner's manual & technical report* (3rd ed.). Kaplan Early Learning.	https://www.kaplanco.com/
Mullen Scales of Early Learning	Mullen, E. M. (1995). *Mullen Scales of Early Learning* (AGS ed.). Pearson.	https://www.pearsonassessments.com/
Parents' Evaluation of Developmental Status	Glascoe, F. P. (1997). *Parents' Evaluation of Developmental Status (PEDS)*. Ellsworth & Vandermeer Press.	https://pedstest.com/
Parents' Evaluation of Developmental Status: Developmental Milestones	Glascoe, F. P., & Robertshaw, N.S. (2007). *PEDS: Developmental Milestones*. Ellsworth & Vandermeer Press.	https://pedstest.com/
Promoting Emergence of Advanced Knowledge Relational Training	Dixon, M. R. (2019). *PEAK Comprehensive Assessment: Administration manual*. Shawnee Scientific Press.	https://www.peak2aba.com/

Questions About Behavioral Function	Matson, J. L., & Vollmer, T. R. (1995). *User's guide: Questions About Behavioral Function (QABF)*. Scientific Publishers.	http://www.disability consultants.org/
Verbal Behavior Milestones Assessment and Placement Program	Sundberg, M. L. (2014). *Verbal behavior milestones assessment and placement program: The VB-MAPP* (2nd ed.). AVB Press.	https://avb press.com/
Vineland Adaptive Behavior Scales	Sparrow, S. S., Cicchetti, D. V., & Saulnier, C. A. (2016). *Vineland-3: Vineland Adaptive Behavior Scales* (3rd ed.). Pearson.	https://www.pearsonassess ments.com/

Bibliography

Abrahams, R., & Groysberg, B. (2021, December 21). How to become a better listener. *Harvard Business Review.* https://hbr.org/2021/12/how-to-become-a-better-listener

Allen, J., Costello, S., & King, A. (2021). *Manage your time like it's all you've got: Behavioral tools that get stuff done.* KeyPress Publishing.

American Psychiatric Association. (2022). *Diagnostic and statistical manual of mental disorders* (5th ed. Text Revision). American Psychiatric Association Publishing.

Angelou, M. (2014). *Rainbow in the cloud: The wisdom and spirit of Maya Angelou.* Random House.

Barrish, H. H., Saunders, M., & Wolf, M. M. (1969). Good behavior game: Effects of individual contingencies for group consequences on disruptive behavior in a classroom. *Journal of Applied Behavior Analysis, 2,* 119–124. https://doi.org/10.1901/jaba.1969.2-119

Behavior Analyst Certification Board. (n.d.). *Board Certified Behavior Analyst.* https://www.bacb.com/bcba/

Brodhead, M. T. (2015). Maintaining professional relationships in an interdisciplinary setting: Strategies for navigating nonbehavioral treatment recommendations for individuals with autism. *Behavior Analysis in Practice, 8*(1), 70–78. https://doi.org/10.1007/s40617-015-0042-7

Bryden, D. P. (1986). The Devil's casebook. *Constitutional Commentary.* 227. https://scholarship.law.umn.edu/concomm/227

Carr, J. E., & Burkholder, E. O. (1998). Creating single-subject design graphs with Microsoft Excel™. *Journal of Applied Behavior Analysis, 31*(2), 245–251. https://doi.org/10.1901/jaba.1998.31-245

Center for Parent Information & Resources. (2022, April). *The short-and-sweet IEP overview.* Retrieved April 3, 2023, from https://www.parentcenterhub.org/iep-overview/

Centers for Disease Control and Prevention. (2023, February 14). *Developmental monitoring and screening.* https://www.cdc.gov/ncbddd/childdevelopment/screening.html

Clance, P. R. (1985). *The impostor phenomenon: When success makes you feel like a fake.* Bantam Books.

Clance, P. R., & Imes, S. A. (1978). The imposter phenomenon in high achieving women: Dynamics and therapeutic intervention. *Psychotherapy: Theory, Research & Practice, 15*(3), 241–247. https://doi.org/10.1037/h0086006

Cooper, J. O., Heron, T. E., & Heward, W. L. (2020). *Applied behavior analysis* (3rd ed.). Pearson.

Daniels, A. C. (2000). *Bringing out the best in people: How to apply the astonishing power of positive reinforcement* (New & Updated ed.). McGraw-Hill.

Daniels, A. C. (2007). *Other people's habits: How to use positive reinforcement to bring out the best in people around you.* Performance Management Publications.

Daniels, A. C., & Bailey, J. S. (2014). *Performance management: Changing behavior that drives organizational effectiveness* (5th ed.). Performance Management Publications.

de Groot, A. D. (1978). *Thought and choice in chess* (2nd ed.). Mouton.

DeVeney, S. L., Cabbage, K., & Mourey, T. (2020). Target selection considerations for speech sound disorder intervention in schools. *Perspectives of the ASHA Special Interest Groups, 5*(6), 1722–1734. https://doi.org/10.1044/2020_persp-20-00138

Dixon, M. R., Jackson, J. W., Small, S. L., Horner-King, M. J., Lik, N. M., Garcia, Y., & Rosales, R. (2009). Creating single-subject design graphs in Microsoft Excel 2007. *Journal of Applied Behavior Analysis, 42*(2), 277–293. https://doi.org/10.1901/jaba.2009.42-277

Donaldson, A. L., & Stahmer, A. C. (2014). Team collaboration: The use of behavior principles for serving students with ASD. *Language, Speech, and Hearing Services in Schools, 45*(4), 261–276. https://doi.org/10.1044/2014_LSHSS-14-0038

Dorey, N. R., Rosales-Ruiz, J., Smith, R., & Lovelace B. (2009). Functional analysis and treatment of self-injury in a captive olive baboon. *Journal of Applied Behavior Analysis, 42*(4), 785–794. https://doi.org/10.1901/jaba.2009.42-785

Drossel, C., & Trahan, M. A. (2015). Behavioral interventions are first-line treatments for managing changes associated with cognitive decline. *The Behavior Therapist, 38*(5), 126–131.

Fisher, J. E., Harsin, C. W., & Hayden, J. E. (2000). Behavioral interventions for patients with dementia. In V. Molinari (Ed.), *Professional psychology in long term care: A comprehensive guide* (pp. 179–200). Hatherleigh Press.

Freudenberger, H. J. (1974). Staff burn-out. *Journal of Social Issues, 30*(1), 159–165. https://doi.org/10.1111/j.1540-4560.1974.tb00706.x

Godley, S. H., Smith, J. E., Passetti, L. L., & Subramaniam, G. (2014). The adolescent community reinforcement approach (A-CRA) as a model paradigm for the management of adolescents with substance use disorders and co-occurring psychiatric disorders. *Substance Abuse, 35*(4), 352–363. https://doi.org/10.1080/08897077.2014.936993

Gupta, S. (2015). Contingency management: Why it pays to quit. *Nature, 522*(7557), S57–S59. https://doi.org/10.1038/522S57a

Halle, T., Zaslow, M., Wessel, J., Moodie, S., & Darling-Churchill, K. (2011, June). *Understanding and choosing assessments and developmental screeners for young children ages 3–5: Profiles of selected measures.* U.S. Department of Health and Human Services. https://www.acf.hhs.gov/opre/report/understanding-and-choosing-assessments-and-developmental-screeners-young-children-ages

Harris, D. L., & Bordere, T. C. (Eds.). (2016). *Handbook of social justice in loss and grief: Exploring diversity, equity, and inclusion.* Routledge.

Harris, S. L., & Weiss, M. J. (2007). *Right from the start: Behavioral intervention for young children with autism* (2nd ed.). Woodbine House.

Herrity, J. (2022, December 20). *9 key steps for conflict resolution at work*. Indeed. https://www.indeed.com/career-advice/career-development/conflict-resolution-at-work

Heward, W. L., Heron, T. E., Neef, N. A., Peterson, S. M., Sainato, D. M., Cartledge, G., Gardner III, R., Peterson, L. D., Hersh, S. B., & Dardig, J. C. (Eds.). (2005). *Focus on behavior analysis in education: Achievements, challenges, and opportunities*. Merrill/ Prentice Hall.

Hibberd, J. (2019). *The imposter cure: Escape the mind-trap of imposter syndrome*. Aster.

Higgins, S. T., Silverman, K., & Heil, S. H. (Eds.). (2008). *Contingency management in substance abuse treatment*. Guilford Press.

Horne, P. J., Tapper, K., Lowe, C. F., Hardman, C. A., Jackson, M. C., & Woolner, J. (2004). Increasing children's fruit and vegetable consumption: A peer-modelling and rewards-based intervention. *European Journal of Clinical Nutrition, 58*(12), 1649–1660. https://doi.org/10.1038/sj.ejcn.1602024

Hovell, M. F., Wahlgren, D. R., & Gehrman, C. A. (2002). The behavioral ecological model: Integrating public health and behavioral science. In R. J. DiClemente, R. A. Crosby, & M. C. Kegler (Eds.), *Emerging theories in health promotion practice and research: Strategies for improving public health* (pp. 347–385). Jossey-Bass.

Huff, D. (1954/1993). *How to lie with statistics* (I. Gies, Illus.). W. W. Norton.

Iliffe, S., & Manthorpe, J. (2019). Burnout may be serious, but what is it? *BMJ: British Medical Journal, 365*, l2108. https://doi.org/10.1136/bmj.l2108

Journal of Applied Behavior Analysis. (n.d.). *Author guidelines*. Wiley Online Library. Retrieved April 3, 2023, from https://onlinelibrary.wiley.com/page/journal/19383703/homepage/forauthors.html

Kawa, S., & Giordano, J. (2012). A brief historicity of the *Diagnostic and Statistical Manual of Mental Disorders*: Issues and implications for the future of psychiatric canon and practice. *Philosophy, Ethics, and Humanities in Medicine, 7*, Article 2. https://doi.org/10.1186/1747-5341-7-2

Keller, F. S. (1968). "Good-bye, teacher ..." *Journal of Applied Behavior Analysis, 1*, 79–89. https://doi.org/10.1901/jaba.1968.1-79

Kelly, A., & Tincani, M. (2013). Collaborative training and practice among applied behavior analysts who support individuals with autism spectrum disorder. *Education and Training in Autism and Developmental Disabilities, 48*(1), 120–131. https://www.jstor.org/stable/23879891

Kisker, E. E., Boller, K., Cabili, C., Nagatoshi, C., Kamler, C., Johnson, C. J., Xue, Y., Esposito, A. M., Henderson, J., Asheer, S., Sciarrino, C., Jethwani, V., Zavitsky, T., Ford, M., & Love, J. M. (2011, April). *Resources for measuring services and outcomes in head start programs serving infants and toddlers*. U.S. Department of Health and Human Services. https://www.acf.hhs.gov/opre/report/resources-measuring-services-and-outcomes-head-start-programs-serving-infants-and

Kubina, R. (2015, October 20). A Standard Celeration Chart projects social behavior outcomes. CentralReach. https://centralreach.com/a-standard-celeration-chart-projects-social-behavior-outcomes/

Kurti, A. N., & Dallery, J. (2013). Internet-based contingency management increases walking in sedentary adults. *Journal of Applied Behavior Analysis, 46*(3), 568–581. https://doi.org/10.1002/jaba.58

Lastovkova, A., Carder, M., Rasmussen, H. M., Sjoberg, L., de Groene, G. J., Sauni, R., Vevoda, J., Vevodova, S., Lasfargues, G., Svartengren, M., Varga, M., Colosio, C., & Pelclova, D. (2018). Burnout syndrome as an occupational disease in the European Union: An exploratory study. *Industrial Health, 56*(2), 160–165. https://doi.org/10.2486/indhealth.2017-0132

LeBlanc, L. A., & Gillis, J. (2012). Behavioral interventions for children with autism spectrum disorders. *Pediatric Clinics of North America, 59*, 147–164. https://doi.org/10.1016/j.pcl.2011.10.006

LeBlanc, L. A., Raetz, P. B., & Feliciano, L. (2011). Behavioral gerontology. In W. W. Fisher, C. C. Piazza, & H. S. Roane (Eds.), *Handbook of applied behavior analysis* (pp. 472–488). The Guilford Press.

Mark, G. (2023). *Attention span: A groundbreaking way to restore balance, happiness and productivity.* Hanover Square Press.

Martin, A. L., Bloomsmith, M. A., Kelley, M. E., Marr, M. J., & Maple, T. L. (2011). Functional analysis and treatment of human-directed undesirable behavior by a captive chimpanzee. *Journal of Applied Behavior Analysis, 44*(1), 139–143. https://doi.org/10.1901/jaba.2011.44-139

Maslach, C., Jackson, S. E., & Leiter, M. P. (2018). *Maslach burnout inventory manual* (4th ed.). Mind Garden.

Maurice, C., Green, G., & Luce, S. C. (Eds.). (1996). *Behavioral intervention for young children with autism: A manual for parents and professionals.* PRO-ED.

McDougale, C. B., Richling, S. M., Longino, E. B., & O'Rourke, S. A. (2020). Mastery criteria and maintenance: A descriptive analysis of applied research procedures. *Behavior Analysis in Practice, 13*(2), 402–410. https://doi.org/10.1007/s40617-019-00365-2

McSween, T. E., & Hockman, A. S. (in press). *The new values-based safety: Using behavioral science to improve your safety culture.* KeyPress Publishing.

Microsoft. (n.d.). *Save a workbook as a template.* Retrieved April 3, 2023, from https://tinyurl.com/4w8dytd8

Moodie, S., Daneri, P., Goldhagen, S., Halle, T., Green, K., & LaMonte, L. (2014, February). *Early childhood developmental screening: A compendium of measures for children ages birth to five.* U.S. Department of Health and Human Services. https://www.acf.hhs.gov/opre/report/early-childhood-developmental-screening-compendium-measures-children-ages-birth-five

Müller-Leonhardt, A., Mitchell, S. G., Vogt, J., & Schürmann, T. (2014). Critical incident stress management (CISM) in complex systems: Cultural adaptation and safety impacts in healthcare. *Accident Analysis & Prevention, 68*, 172–180. https://doi.org/10.1016/j.aap.2013.12.018

Normand, M. P., Dallery, J., & Ong, T. (2015). Applied behavior analysis for health and fitness. In H. S. Roane, J. E. Ringdahl, & T. S. Falcomata (Eds.), *Clinical and organizational applications of applied behavior analysis* (pp. 555–582). Academic Press.

Normand, M. P., Dallery, J., & Slanzi, C. M. (2021). Leveraging applied behavior analysis research and practice in the service of public health. *Journal of Applied Behavior Analysis, 54*(2), 457–483. https://doi.org/10.1002/jaba.832

Office of Special Education and Rehabilitative Services. (2000). *A guide to the individualized education program.* U.S. Department of Education. https://www2.ed.gov/parents/needs/speced/iepguide/iepguide.pdf

Petry, N. M., Barry, D., Pescatello, L., & White, W. B. (2011). A low-cost reinforcement procedure improves short-term weight loss outcomes. *The American Journal of Medicine, 124*(11), 1082–1085. https://doi.org/10.1016/j.amjmed.2011.04.016

Poling, A., Weetjens, B. J., Cox, C., Mgode, G., Jubitana, M., Kazwala, R., Mfinanga, G. S., & Veld, D. H. (2010). Using giant African pouched rats to detect tuberculosis in human sputum samples: 2009 findings. *The American Journal of Tropical Medicine and Hygiene, 83*(6), 1308–1310. https://doi.org/10.4269/ajtmh.2010.10-0180

Sakulku, J., & Alexander, J. (2011). The impostor phenomenon. *International Journal of Behavioral Science, 6*(1), 73–92. https://doi.org/10.14456/ijbs.2011.6

Samra, R. (2018). Brief history of burnout. *BMJ: British Medical Journal, 363,* k5268. https://doi.org/10.1136/bmj.k5268

Samra, R. (2019). Author's reply to Iliffe and Manthorpe. *BMJ: British Medical Journal, 365,* l2195. https://doi.org/10.1136/bmj.l2195

Schaufeli, W. B. (2017). Burnout: A short socio-cultural history. In S. Neckel, A. K. Schaffner, & G. Wagner (Eds.), *Burnout, fatigue, exhaustion: An interdisciplinary perspective on a modern affliction* (pp. 105–127). Palgrave Macmillan. https://doi.org/10.1007/978-3-319-52887-8_5

Schaufeli, W. B., Leiter, M. P., & Maslach, C. (2009). Burnout: 35 years of research and practice. *Career Development International, 14*(3), 204–220. https://doi.org/10.1108/13620430910966406

Schindler, J. (2019, August 6). The skill of workplace negotiation. *Forbes.* https://www.forbes.com/sites/forbescoachescouncil/2019/08/06/the-skill-of-workplace-negotiation/?sh=32ce9ccc2595

Simon, H. A., & Chase, W. G. (1973). Skill in chess: Experiments with chess-playing tasks and computer simulation of skilled performance throw light on some human perceptual and memory processes. *American Scientist, 61*(4), 394–403. http://www.jstor.org/stable/27843878

Skinner, B. F. (1956). A case history in scientific method. *American Psychologist, 11*(5), 221–233. https://so06.tci-thaijo.org/index.php/IJBS/article/view/521

Skinner B. F. (1957). *Verbal behavior.* Prentice Hall.

Slowiak, J. M., & DeLongchamp, A. C. (2022). Self-care strategies and job-crafting practices among behavior analysts: Do they predict perceptions of work-life balance, work engagement, and burnout? *Behavior Analysis in Practice, 15*(2), 414–432. https://doi.org/10.1007/s40617-021-00570-y

Standard Celeration Society. (n.d.). *Standard Celeration Charting resources*. Retrieved April 3, 2023, from https://celeration.org/freeresources/

Sundberg, M. L. (2014). *Verbal behavior milestones assessment and placement program: The VB-MAPP* (2nd ed.). AVB Press.

U.S. Department of Education. (n.d.-a). *Individuals with Disabilities Education Act: Topic areas*. https://sites.ed.gov/idea/topic-areas/

U.S. Department of Education. (n.d.-b). *Laws & guidance*. Retrieved April 3, 2023, from https://www2.ed.gov/policy/landing.jhtml

Welp, A., Meier, L. L., & Manser, T. (2015). Emotional exhaustion and workload predict clinician-rated and objective patient safety. *Frontiers of Psychology*, 5(1573). https://doi.org/10.3389/fpsyg.2014.01573

West, C. P., Dyrbye, L. N., Erwin, P. J., & Shanafelt, T. D. (2016). Interventions to prevent and reduce physician burnout: A systematic review and meta-analysis. *The Lancet, 388*(10057), 2272–2281. https://doi.org/10.1016/S0140-6736(16)31279-X

West, C. P., Dyrbye, L. N., & Shanafelt, T. D. (2018). Physician burnout: Contributors, consequences and solutions. *Journal of Internal Medicine, 283*(6), 516–529. https://doi.org/10.1111/joim.12752

Woo, M., & Bacon, O. (2020). Alarm fatigue. In Abt Associates, Inc., *Making healthcare safer III: A critical analysis of existing and emerging patient safety practices* (pp. 13-1–13-17). Agency for Healthcare Research and Quality. https://www.ncbi.nlm.nih.gov/books/NBK555522/

Woolridge, S. (2023, April 12). *Writing respectfully: Person-first and identity-first language*. National Institutes of Health. https://www.nih.gov/about-nih/what-we-do/science-health-public-trust/perspectives/writing-respectfully-person-first-identity-first-language

World Health Organization. (2019, May 28). Burn-out an "occupational phenomenon": International classification of diseases. https://www.who.int/news/item/28-05-2019-burn-out-an-occupational-phenomenon-international-classification-of-diseases

Young, V. (2023). *The secret thoughts of successful women: And men: Why capable people suffer from impostor syndrome and how to thrive in spite of it*. Currency.

Index

Acknowledgments

This book has been brought to you by ...

Ashley Johnson, editor extraordinaire

I would like to extend my special thanks and gratitude to my editor, Ashley Johnson. Her time, attention, and encouragement kept this project going while her ideas shaped it into what you see today.

Contributors:

Amber Stanley, MS, BCBA

Cassie McKeel, MS, BCBA

Thomas Freeman, MS, BCBA

Thank you for your contributions and support of the project. Your perspectives and knowledge were invaluable additions.

Jana Burtner, lead designer

Thank you to Jana for the tireless work of creating over 200 design elements. Thank you for your patience both in coming on mid-project and for the monotony of placing 137 lines. You've brought the book to life.

KaCee Costello-Vargo, cover designer

Thank you to KaCee for the beautiful design on the front, back, and spine. You've made our project feel like a real book.

My family and friends

Thank you for all of the support, being with me through all of the ups, downs, and late nights. Thank you for picking up all of the balls I dropped and listening to me talk about nothing but this book for a year.

And "viewers" like you

Thank you for reading! Thank you for all the work you do and will continue to do in behavior analysis. I hope you continue to grow and develop, and that you bring the field along as you do.

About the Author

Mariah began her professional career as a classical musician. When Mariah's son was diagnosed with autism, she put her French horn career on the shelf to learn how to better help him. When many people told her what her son's limitations would be, Mariah knew that with the right professional care, he could achieve much more.

Helping her son learn to speak and adapt to his environment inspired Mariah to help others. She completed her MA in Applied Behavior Analysis from Ball State University in 2017 and went on to become a BCBA, completing her field experience at Marcus Autism Center.

Her passion for care has led her to a variety of settings like home care, clinics, and schools in Florida and Georgia.

Mariah and her son live in Atlanta and love all that the city has to offer. He currently enjoys learning about flags, and Mariah enjoys knitting and trying to garden.

KeyPress Publishing

We strive to provide individualized services and support to all our authors. Our team of experts is here to answer all your questions and produce your ideal products. We offer personal attention from the time you reach out, through the writing, submission, and review process, close partnerships with our design team to fulfill your visions, and our publishing expertise to help you publish, promote, and sell your book.

A Sample of KeyPress Publications:

ABA Technologies
ACADEMY ®

Offering professional development programs for continuing education and career or personal growth is one way we support our mission and the field of behavior analysis. We offer a superior level of learner focus and instructional design, high-quality content from leading experts in the field, and easy to use platform that allows for learning anytime and easy connections to other learners.

A Sample of ABA Tech Academy Courses:

"I like the module/phase chunking of the course, the recordings, and the interactive question-answer practice. The instructors were enjoyable to listen to, professional, and knowledgeable."

–Stacey, Verified student in the OBM Specialist Certificate course

www.ABATechAcademy.com

www.ingramcontent.com/pod-product-compliance
Lightning Source LLC
Chambersburg PA
CBHW070113030426
42335CB00016B/2140